TIME TO LEAVE

To Dr. Dennis Modry,

a genuine Alberta hero and true Alberta patriot.

Copyright © 2024 by Michael Wagner

All rights reserved. No part of this book may be reproduced in any form by an electronic or mechanical means, including information storage and retrieval systems, without permission in writing from the publisher, except by a reviewer who may quote brief passages in a review.

First Edition Paperback May 2024
ISBN 978-1-7775047-7-9
Published by Domino Effect Publishing, All Rights Reserved

TIME TO LEAVE

Canada Cannot Be Fixed

Table of Contents

7   - Foreword
10 - Preface
12 - Introduction
23 - Chapter 1 – The Energy War of the 1970s
35 - Chapter 2 – The National Energy Program
45 - Chapter 3 - The Western Canada Concept Party of Alberta
62 - Chapter 4 – The Alternatives Have Failed
74 - Chapter 5 - Constitutional Reform is Not Going to Happen
85 - Chapter 6 - The West is Different from the Rest of Canada
97 - Chapter 7 – Fear for the Future
107 - Conclusion
119 - References
125 - About the Author

Foreword

Our federal government believes man is the rival of mankind. Listen to our progressive parliamentarians speak, and you'll comprehend their conviction that Canadians are the rivals of Canada, and provinces are the rivals of the country.

Alberta isn't the only example of what I'm talking about, but it is a prime example. If you ask federal leaders whether they love Alberta, the overwhelming majority of them eagerly say, "yes." But if you ask our leaders whether they love the various freedom groups, peaceful truckers, and conservative families that compose Alberta, they spitefully say, "no."

Let's be more specific. Federal leaders might love Alberta, but they do not love Albertans. Bureaucrats come into the light to receive Alberta's magnificent resources, economic fuel, and monetary muscle, but they retreat to the political shadows when those who harvest the oil, pay the taxes, and provide the wealth, voice their present concerns.

Therefore, we are challenged with a problem, not merely aesthetic or superficial, as old as the province itself: Ottawa's trying to turn Alberta into something anti-Albertan. A devastating Trojan horse, siphoning power from the provinces, and injecting it into the federal government's veins, has been programmed into the structure of our country.

I've heard some people say it's too late for Alberta, and that it's been consumed by the massive maw of Ottawa. I've heard others try to pacify the situation, speaking like nothing's wrong between this solitary province and the federal government. Both visions of reality are false, and indulging them will only lead to the House of Commons conquering every acre of our country.

Instead, we must defend our Alberta, not because it's perfect, but because it's our own. The Canadian Government's inverted our values, laws, rights, and freedoms; Alberta's independence can flip them right-side up.

There are few men able to detail the reasons, procedures, and logic, for pursuing Alberta's independence, as eloquently as Dr. Michael Wagner. He is, without a doubt, the humblest intellectual I've ever met. His research is honest, his writing is precise, and his reasoning for Alberta's independence from Canada is clear.

But in Dr. Wagner exists that unique and rare ability to bridge what seem to be unbridgeable gaps. Many people think that the relationship between Ottawa and Alberta is irreconcilable. Their passion for their province, or their defence of their country, leads to inflammatory accusations that leave both sides furious and fruitless. *Time To Leave* however, provides us with an alternative.

Dr. Wagner's cool style presents an earnest desire to solve the problems between Alberta and Canada, without spewing radical ideals. Not only are his arguments grounded in truth, but his writing is structured in such a way that even a dissenting side is able to say, "I understand your position. Your reasons for wanting to be independent are justified."

From his latest work, I learned a powerful political paradox: Alberta's independence won't break our relationship with Canada; Alberta's independence will fix it.

It's because components in an engine move independently of each other that they're able to move at all. Neighbours are friendly because they can close their doors. Families stay close by giving each other space, and tensions between the east and west will relax when they're no longer fighting for power and control.

We tend to worry that Alberta's independence would guarantee hostile relations with Canada, but the truth is very much the opposite. The relations between Alberta and Ottawa are hostile *right now*. Everything we try to do is blocked by federal leaders. Our requests for new pipelines are closed, our demands for financial fairness are denied, and our negotiations for equality in the federal government have been extinguished.

By now, the solution to our problem is clear. We have to move out of this house, and into a new home with our own rights, freedoms, and autonomy. Greater independence is needed, not only for Alberta, but for all provinces across Canada. The more independence there is, the stronger, freer, and more stable the nation will be. Our previous paradox, therefore, is resolved. Alberta's struggle for independence isn't just for Alberta. It's for Canada.

Tanner L. Hnidey, independent economist

Blackfoot, Alberta

Preface

In 2009 I wrote a history of the Alberta independence movement entitled *Alberta: Separatism Then and Now*. When it appeared, there were hardly any sales and it looked like a wasted effort.

Thanks to Justin Trudeau's election victory in 2015, however, interest in the book began to materialize. During a series of Wexit meetings in the fall of 2019, a few hundred of copies were sold.

Subsequently, some people asked me to update it. Rather than that, I decided to write a new book that became *No Other Option: Self-Determination for Alberta*. Although this book included a short chapter updating the history of the movement, its main thrust was to argue that Alberta should become independent.

At the time, I thought it would be my last book on Alberta independence.

However, over the last two years, as I have continued researching this issue, I have come across additional materials that help to substantiate the independence option. Ultimately,

I decided to write another book to explain how this material helps to support the case for Alberta independence.

The more I learn about Alberta's history, the stronger the case for independence looks. In presenting this information, I hope others will reach the same conclusion.

Many Albertans already know that their province is mistreated within Canada. They want something to change. Only a minority, however, seem to favour independence. Instead, most people want the country to be reformed so that Alberta will be taken seriously at the national level.

After studying the province's history for years, though, I find this line of thinking to be ill-informed.

Over a period of decades, many Albertans have worked hard for the kinds of changes that would benefit their province. In spite of great efforts, none of these changes were accomplished due to Canada's existing political system.

Nor do I believe any of the hoped-for changes can ever be accomplished. The lesson of the last fifty years is that Canada cannot be reformed in a way that will benefit Alberta. Therefore, the only viable option is independence.

With this book – as with *No Other Option* – I hope to convince more Albertans to embrace that conclusion. Whether readers agree or not, I think they will understand that the case for Alberta separating from Canada is based upon solid historical research and thinking.

Michael Wagner

Edmonton, Alberta

Introduction

After decades of futile efforts to reform Canada, it is now time for Alberta to strike out on its own to form a new, independent country.

The case for Alberta independence can be best understood by looking at the province's history. For generations, Albertans have felt ignored or even exploited within Canada, and eventually this feeling has reached the point where some believe the only solution is to form a new country.

Right from the time it annexed the prairie West, Canada's central government has been largely indifferent to the concerns of Westerners. At the time of annexation, Canada ignored the interests of prairie residents until it faced armed resistance. Events since that time reveal a consistent pattern of Ottawa disregarding the West unless it faced determined opposition it could not avoid. That is the lesson of history, and Westerners should learn from history.

The Canadian prairies were originally part of Rupert's Land, the Hudson Bay drainage basin that was administered by the Hudson's Bay Company for 200 years (1670-1870). The company had a monopoly on the region's fur trade – a very profitable industry at that time.

By 1868, efforts were underway to transfer Rupert's Land to the Dominion of Canada. Then, in "December 1869 a Canadian governor was sent, proclaiming his authority over the West. At no time were the inhabitants of the region consulted" (Conway 2014, 29).

However, the mostly-Métis inhabitants of the Red River settlement were not about to quietly acquiesce to Canada's rule. White settlers and the Métis shared a concern that their rights, particularly land rights, would be overridden without prior guarantees. Both wanted some form of responsible government and the prospect of exchanging the unhappy but known dictatorship of the Company for the distant and unknown dictatorship of Canada was viewed with some alarm (Conway 2014, 29).

The settlers formed a provisional government under Louis Riel to represent their interests. Riel's supporters had guns and weren't afraid to use them. To appease the Red River inhabitants, the Canadian government created the province of Manitoba to give those people a better political status within their new country.

However, unlike other provinces, Manitoba did not receive control over its land and resources. When Alberta and Saskatchewan were formed in 1905, they too, were denied control of their land and resources. This situation was not rectified until 1930 when all three provinces were granted such control.

Prominent historian W. L. Morton of Manitoba made no bones about the fact that the West had been unfairly treated by Canada. "The resistance of the Metis," he wrote, "set a tradition at work, the tradition of western grievance. The struggle of the prairie west against political subordination to central Canada had begun" (Morton 1980, 150).

As noted previously, right from the beginning of Canadian involvement on the prairies, Western interests were disregarded until Westerners actively resisted the central government. This would be the pattern for the next 150 years or more.

To this day, Westerners must push back forcefully or they will be crushed by Ottawa's indifference to their concerns.

According to Morton, the main impetus driving the formation and growth of Canada was the "Laurentian thesis." Canada, in this view, was forged primarily by the commercial system of the St. Lawrence region.

From this perspective, the goal of creating wealth for central Canada has been the main reason for the West's unjust treatment. As Morton put it, "Confederation was brought about to increase the wealth of central Canada, and until that original purpose is altered, and the concentration of wealth and population by national policy in central Canada ceases, Confederation must remain an instrument of injustice" (Morton 1980, 108).

In other words, the structure of Confederation was unjust to the West right from the very beginning. Morton explains that "the West was annexed to Confederation as a subordinate region and so remained for sixty years. Such was the historical schooling of the West. It had, therefore, to fight its way up to self-government and equality in Confederation; nor is the process ended" (Morton 1980, 109).

Morton points out that all the West really wanted was to be an equal partner within Canada, rather than having second-class status as a region. As he put it, "The prairie west has been defined as a colonial society seeking equality in Confederation. That equality was sought in order that the West should be like, not different from, the rest of Canada" (Morton 1980, 159).

George Koch picks up on this same equality-seeking theme and explains how it led to efforts to improve the West's status within Canada. He begins by noting the West's original subordinate status within Canada:

> For 35 years after the Hudson's Bay territory was acquired by Canada, and effectively for decades thereafter, the Prairies were in every sense Canada's colony. This was no happenstance. They were conceived specifically to fulfill that role. In the Quebec Resolutions, in the Confederation debates, in John A. Macdonald's letters and pronouncements, the western interior was viewed as a means to enrich central Canada. Settlement, development, the CPR, Indian policy and local government were all planned with this in mind (Koch 1991, 282).

This meant that the West's role was essentially to produce resources and staples that could be utilized and consumed by central Canada. As Morton had mentioned, even after Alberta and Saskatchewan were formed in 1905, their lands and resources remained under federal control until 1930.

As immigrants were brought in to populate the prairies, pioneer the land and create an agricultural economy, these new settlers soon
> found themselves locked into enduring conflict with

Ottawa. The West wanted responsible government; Ottawa sought to sustain colonial despotism. The West wanted commercial freedom; Ottawa pushed protectionism. The West liked populism and political pragmatism; Ottawa depended upon national partisanship and, later, upon executive federalism (Koch 1991, 284).

Despite this conflict, Westerners did not desire independence from Canada. Rather than separatism, they looked for other solutions that would essentially make them genuine participants in Canadian national affairs.

One seeming exception to this is Alwyn Bramley-Moore, a Liberal MLA in Alberta from 1909-1913. In 1911, during his time in office, he wrote a book about Alberta's subservient place in Confederation entitled, *Canada and Her Colonies: Or Home Rule for Alberta*. He wanted to rouse Albertans to demand that the federal government give the province control of its own resources. Since none of the three prairie provinces had been given control of their natural resources when they entered Confederation, he considered Alberta to be a "colony" of Canada.

The Alberta government of that time was largely dependent on annual subsidies from the federal government for its revenue. The federal government received large royalties from Alberta's resources, and returned some money to the province in compensation. The subsidy was insufficient to cover the provinces expenses, and Bramley-Moore dismissed it as "pocket-money." However, he believed that if Alberta controlled the resources and received the royalties, its financial situation would be much stronger.

To correct the situation, he proposed that Albertans take various measures to gain control of their resources. First of all, the province should appeal to the Imperial Parliament in London, England "to redress her wrongs" (Bramley-Moore 1911, 148).

Secondly, Alberta's seven members of Parliament should band together "to harass the Central Government on every possible occasion, to expose her perfidious practices, and to cheer any reverses Fate might have in store for her" (Bramley-Moore 1911, 149).

Thirdly, children in the schools should "be taught to regard this Canada, this stepmother, as the incarnation of greed, tyranny and oppression" (Bramley-Moore 1911, 149).

And as a last resort, Bramley-Moore proposed the nuclear option – declaring independence: "A radical procedure, and rather a practical one in its way, would be to hoist the flag of independence, which would *ipso facto* make the province owner of her own resources" (Bramley-Moore 1911, 150).

However, this was not the ultimate goal he desired. Instead, it was a step to strengthen Alberta's position to renegotiate a better deal with Canada. For as he wrote,
After a banquet or two and patriotic oratory the province might express a desire to be reinstated in the Confederation, and then she would be in a position to make a bargain. This seems the most sensible plan; there is no objection to forming a partnership with the Confederation, but there is an objection to being used as a step-child and deprived of local autonomy (Bramley-Moore 1911, 150).

In other words, Alberta would declare independence as a way to gain control of its resources, then rejoin Confederation on better terms. Justice for Alberta, rather than independence, was Bramley-Moore's ultimate goal.

Therefore, Koch is correct when he writes, "Fundamentally, westerners of the 19th century, like those of the 20th, wanted an equal part in national life. As a whole they never were, and did not become, separatists. They wanted justice, not independence. Neither did they ever seriously favour annexation by the United States." (Koch 1991, 284).

Despite their opposition to joining the United States, however, many Westerners admired the American political system because it gave the less populated states equal representation with the more populated states in the Senate.

To use Ted Byfield's term, the Americans had a "Triple-E" Senate. That is, a Senate with an Equal number of senators from each state, where the members are Elected and have Effective political powers.

Supposedly the Canadian Senate was created to offer a voice for regional representation as well, but it completely failed in this function. "From the start," Koch writes, "that body was regarded with scorn in the West. As early as the 1890s, westerners were demanding it be changed" (Koch 1991, 284).

Furthermore, early in the twentieth century Westerners learned that they could not get their concerns addressed by working within the national Liberal or Conservative parties. As a result, they created their
> own political movements to attack the institutional inequities directly. This spirit would rise again and again throughout the coming century, both in the

form of populist, western-based, so-called protest movements, and as powerful provincial governments taking an active role in national affairs (Koch 1991, 284).

At the time Koch was writing in 1991, the Reform Party of Canada was rapidly gaining support in western Canada. During the 1990s it achieved considerable success in the West, including winning the vast majority of Alberta's seats in the 1993 and 1997 federal elections.

Despite this success, however, the Reform Party never came close to achieving its goal of reforming Canada's national institutions to get a bigger voice for the West, namely, through the creation of a Triple-E Senate.

What this means is that Westerners – and particularly Albertans – have already spent considerable time and effort trying to improve their political situation within Canada. Yet, after all this time, Alberta is still having harmful policies imposed on it by a hostile federal government.

So here we are still spinning our wheels.

This means that the time for patiently working on a solution with Ottawa is over.

Which brings us to the purpose of this book. Since we learn from history that efforts to reform Canada for the benefit of Alberta have been tried but cannot succeed due to the political system, independence appears to be the only way out.

That is, the only way to bring this long conflict to an end is for Alberta to move towards independence. A successful independence referendum will make Albertans "masters in our own home" – to borrow a phrase from Quebec – and enable us to make the best decisions for our future.

Although there has been conflict between central Canada and the West since the late nineteenth century, the most intense conflict really began in 1973 due to the energy crisis. Chapter 1 describes the reaction of the federal government and Ontario to the rise in oil prices, and their desire to seize Alberta's oil wealth for the benefit of "all Canadians," i.e., central Canadians. This conflict led to the origin of Alberta's separatist movement.

The battles over oil pricing and control between Alberta and Ottawa during the 1970s were a prelude to the federal government's most vicious assault on Alberta's resources in the 1980 National Energy Program (NEP). Chapter 2 examines the NEP and the effect it had on Alberta.

The NEP led to tremendous growth in the Alberta separatist movement. The most important organization in that movement, the Western Canada Concept Party of Alberta (WCC), elected an MLA to the Alberta Legislature in a 1982 by-election. The WCC is also noteworthy because one of its founders, Dr. Ruth Gorman, actively campaigned against Pierre Trudeau's so-called *Charter of Rights and Freedoms*. She accurately identified the Charter's deliberate failure to protect property rights as a major threat to the rights of Canadians and Westerners in particular. This is the topic of Chapter 3.

For various reasons the WCC began to decline, so patriotic Albertans pinned their hopes on Brian Mulroney's Progressive Conservative Party in the 1984 election to oust the Liberals and redress Alberta's grievances. On top of that, the idea of Senate reform – especially a "Triple-E" Senate – captured the imagination of many Westerners as a way to balance the federation. Unfortunately, due to the dominance of central Canada, Mulroney could not give the West what it needed, and Senate reform along the lines desired by many Westerners was a non-starter. These matters are covered in Chapter 4.

One of the founding members of the Reform Party of Canada – Stephen Harper – became leader of the Conservative Party of Canada and then prime minister of the country. Harper had a sincere desire to enact Senate reform but was hampered by various factors and eventually blocked by the Supreme Court of Canada. Overall, due to the dominance of the "Laurentian Consensus," Harper could do little for the West. Chapter 5 describes these efforts and how they show that Canada cannot be reformed to benefit Alberta, even when one of its champions is prime minister.

In some respects the West – and especially Alberta – is culturally different from the rest of Canada. One manifestation of this difference is the aspect of political culture described – for better or worse – as "western alienation." This is the topic of Chapter 6.

Some people argue that any moves towards independence will harm Alberta by chasing away business, as Quebec experienced in the 1970s when the Parti Québécois came to power. Also, there are those who say that Alberta should co-operate in phasing out its oil industry to save the world from climate change. These issues are addressed in Chapter 7.

Finally, in the Conclusion, it is argued that in light of past failed efforts to reform Canada for the benefit of Alberta, independence is the only viable path forward. Canada's constitutional law allows provinces to pursue independence through a clearly-worded referendum receiving a clear majority vote. There is no reason this process can't be successfully followed by Alberta.

In sum, this book provides clear reasoning to justify Alberta becoming an independent country. From my perspective, this is the inescapable conclusion from a consideration of the province's history.

Chapter 1 –
The Energy War of the 1970s

During the first decades of its existence, Alberta was a relatively poor province within Canada. That began to change when oil was discovered near Leduc in 1947. From that moment onward, the production of oil and natural gas would become the dominant feature of Alberta's economy and eventually result in Alberta becoming the richest province in the country.

However, until 1973, the price of oil was low and so the economic benefits to Alberta were not huge. That year marked a turning point, though, for two reasons. First, the federal government began to claim a larger share of revenue from Alberta's oil; and secondly, the price of oil skyrocketed as a result of war in the Middle East.

On October 6, 1973, a coalition of Arab countries launched a surprise attack on Israel in what is known as the Yom Kippur War. The Arab countries were allies of the Soviet Union while Israel was an ally of the United States.

Ultimately, Israel was able to successfully beat back the Arab onslaught.

In 1960, the Organization of the Petroleum Exporting Countries (OPEC) had been formed to influence the global oil market and increase prices. A number of Arab countries were oil exporters and OPEC members. They supported their Arab neighbours' attack on Israel, and this would have momentous consequences for the price of oil. Before the war began, the price of oil was about $3.00 a barrel.

> That soon changed. As Peter Foster writes, OAPEC, the Arab group within OPEC, began openly to discuss using oil as a weapon of war. Shortly afterwards OAPEC met in Kuwait and decided unilaterally to raise the price to $5.12 a barrel, a 70% increase. But worse was to come. On the second day of their meeting, they decided to impose a production cut of 5% monthly until Israel withdrew from what they considered to be Arab lands. At the same time, the Saudi foreign minister was in Washington delivering a similar message. Shortly after the Kuwait meeting, Saudi Arabia announced a 10% production cutback and a total embargo on oil shipments to the United States and the Netherlands (Foster 1979, 25).

As a result of these actions, the price of oil increased rapidly. On January 1, 1974, the price rose to $11.65 a barrel.

Suddenly, Alberta's oil was worth a fortune.

Shortly before the Yon Kippur War, conflict over oil between Alberta and Pierre Trudeau's Liberal government had already begun. On September 13, 1973, Liberal Energy minister Donald Macdonald told Alberta's energy minister,

Bill Dickie, that the federal government was imposing an export tax on oil. It was called an "export levy." This was an unprecedented move.

Premier Peter Lougheed reacted appropriately and forcefully.

> In a speech to the Calgary Chamber of Commerce the following day, Lougheed called the export levy "the most discriminatory action ever taken by a federal government against a particular province in the entire history of confederation . . . Jobs, both existing and future, are in jeopardy in Alberta today . . . We have to try to protect the Alberta public interest – not from the Canadian public interest – but from Central and Eastern Canadian domination of the West" (Foster 1979, 41-42).

Lougheed went on to note that, "The natural resources of the provinces are owned by the provinces under the terms of Confederation. The action taken by Ottawa strikes at the very roots of Confederation" (Wood 1985, 147).

In December, with the oil price rising rapidly, Trudeau announced that his government would create a new national petroleum corporation. He also announced his intention for the federal government to grab more of Alberta's resource revenues, saying, "We do not think it equitable or fair that surplus profits return solely to the provinces producing oil. In the government's opinion, the whole country should take benefit from any windfall profits" (Foster 1979, 42).

Then, on May 6, 1974, federal finance minister John Turner announced a new budget, which included a provision that provincial oil royalties would no longer be deductible for federal tax purposes. In other words, the federal government was going to gouge the oil companies to get more money.

In the five months after this policy was announced, 32 drilling rigs and 600 oil workers left Alberta for the United States (Hustak 1979, 170).

Before it was implemented, however, there was a federal election. The re-elected Trudeau government brought in a new budget that still contained the non-deductibility provisions. But it did contain a few concessions to the oil companies.

Nevertheless, it was very bad for Alberta. As Lougheed explained,

> Mr. Turner very conveniently ignores an export tax of one and a half billion dollars a year from the depleting oil wells of Alberta, wells that may only last for ten years. That takes out of the heritage of Alberta between $800 and $1,000 a year for every man, woman and child in our province. In essence . . . I guess it's probably the biggest ripoff of any province that's ever occurred in Confederation's history (Wood 1985, 155).

Lougheed correctly argued that under Canada's constitution natural resources belong to the provinces and Turner's policies involved an invasion of provincial jurisdiction. As Lougheed stated at the time, "The whole concept of taxing the resources of the province is going to destroy Confederation as we know it. It violates the whole spirit of Confederation" (Hustak 1979, 171).

Back then, the complete extent of Alberta's oil resources was not known. Lougheed was concerned because it seemed the province's oil was rapidly being produced and could run out within a few years. Therefore, it was absolutely essential for Alberta to accumulate as much income from its energy resources as possible, so that the proceeds could be reinvested for the future.

Shortly after Turner's November budget was announced, Don Getty, Alberta's Intergovernmental Affairs Minister, urged Albertans to

> fight an outright battle for the future. If Ottawa does not alter its ways, I would not be part of an Alberta government that would not fight with every weapon at its command. . . . Maybe we will lose. Maybe they can confiscate our dreams and our future, but if they do, let's make sure it is only after we have fought them every inch of the way (Hustak 1979, 173).

It's important to note the Trudeau government mandated that Canadian produced oil (which meant mostly Alberta oil) be sold within Canada at prices much below the world price. Thus, Alberta subsidized oil to the rest of Canada by receiving much less than it ought to have received. Furthermore, oil exported to the United States was sold at world prices, but the federal government took the difference between the Canadian price and the world price on every barrel exported. That was the oil export tax.

As a result of the oil export tax, Trudeau's government raked in huge amounts of money that should have gone to Alberta, because that oil was owned by Alberta under the constitution. Trudeau used that money to subsidize oil imports to eastern Canada.

For example, in 1975 the Canadian price was $7.44 and the world price was $11.35. In 1980, the Canadian price was $17.30 and the world price was $44.66 (Gray 2000, 140). These prices are in Canadian dollars. Clearly, Alberta was getting burned by the federal government through the latter's oil pricing policy.

But as Lougheed correctly pointed out, "If Ontario owned the oil you can be assured that we in Alberta would be buying it at the world price" (Hustak 1979, 228).

University of Regina professor John Conway summarizes the overall situation this way:

> Ottawa imposed an oil price freeze in the fall of 1973, slapped on a federal oil export tax to capture increased revenues, and decided to deny resource companies the right to deduct provincial royalty charges before computing federal taxes. These moves markedly diminished the extent to which the energy provinces could capture the windfall. They were supplemented by a 1974 law granting Ottawa the power to fix oil prices. Further, Ottawa threatened to impose a federal tax on natural gas exports and resisted dramatic increases in natural gas prices in Canada (Conway 2014, 166).

Ontario supported Trudeau against Alberta

Pierre Trudeau was certainly the ringleader in this pillaging of Alberta's oil resources during the 1970s. But what is not so well remembered is that he had notable accomplices. Prominent among those accomplices was Bill Davis, the Progressive Conservative premier of Ontario.

During the 1970s, the Progressive Conservative government of Ontario was one of Alberta's central Canadian enemies. This is because Ontarians felt entitled to Alberta's energy resources at well-below world prices. And indeed, Pierre

Trudeau's government mandated such low prices for central Canada at Alberta's expense.

But Peter Lougheed fought valiantly against Trudeau's discriminatory energy policies, with overwhelming support from Alberta's citizens.

Ontarians did not like that. They were outraged that Albertans expected to be treated as equals within Canada.

For example, in his 1979 book, *Mandate for Canada*, prominent University of Toronto professor John Crispo wrote: "Québec is far from the only threat to the unity of this country. Indeed, at times Alberta appears to be an even greater menace to Confederation. At least, Québec can claim to fear for the loss of its original culture and language. All Alberta seems to care about is control over its resources" (Crispo 1979, 64).

It's certainly true Alberta cared about control over its resources. After all, it was being looted by the federal government, and the proceeds were being distributed – in the form of subsidized energy prices – to central Canadians like Prof. Crispo.

Shortly after oil prices began to skyrocket as a result of the Yom Kippur War, Ontario was already demanding prices substantially below market value for Alberta's oil. Premier Davis was requesting that "part of such huge profits from domestic oil should be used to benefit all Canadians, not just the oil-producing provinces" (Hoy 1985, 339).

But when an Ontario premier refers to "all Canadians," he usually means the inhabitants of the St. Lawrence River valley.

Of course, Lougheed opposed Davis's position. When he rejected an Ontario proposal during negotiations over oil pricing, Ontario Treasurer Frank Miller called Lougheed "a greater threat to Confederation than Québec's René Lévesque" (Hoy 1985, 323). That was a nasty shot because Lévesque was a full-fledged separatist.

Premier Davis essentially declared "open war" on Alberta when he released an official Ontario government document entitled *Oil Pricing and Security: A Policy Framework for Canada* on August 15, 1979. As David Wood points out, "Its proposals were incredibly offensive not just to the Lougheed government but to all Albertans" (Wood 1985, 159).

In this document, the Ontario government claimed to have as much right to set oil pricing in Canada as the federal government. But that wasn't even the worst of it. As Wood explains, "The Davis document recommended closing Alberta's Heritage Fund and shifting new money from provincial royalties into the federal treasury" (Wood 1985, 159-160).

Read that again: Ontario wanted Alberta's oil royalties – the birthright of every Alberta citizen – to be confiscated by the federal government! This was a brazen attack on Alberta's constitutional rights – not by Pierre Trudeau – but by Conservative Premier Davis of Ontario.

> As Wood explains, Lougheed recognized that Ontario's position was a clear attempt to change the basic concept of Confederation in a particularly objectionable way by altering the natural resource ownership rights of provinces only with respect to oil and natural gas, leaving intact a province's ownership

rights over such things as forest products, nickel, water power, and pulp and paper (Wood 1985, 160).

In other words, the natural resources of Ontario would remain in Ontario's hands but Alberta's oil and gas resources would be confiscated by the federal government for the benefit of "all Canadians."

Premier Davis could boost his popularity at home by telling Ontarians "that oil and natural gas were national commodities belonging to all Canadians, and telling eastern manufacturers they should always be able to enjoy cheaper energy (meaning only oil and natural gas)" (Wood 1985, 160).

The Ontario government was very supportive of Pierre Trudeau's confiscation of Alberta's oil revenue. That is to say, "With the full approval of Ontario, Ottawa was systematically denying the western provinces the full control of resources supposedly guaranteed by the Constitution. Davis enjoyed the advantage of watching Ottawa carry out policies nicely tailored to Ontario's needs" (Braid and Sharpe 1990, 144).

Although Trudeau tried to negotiate with Alberta over oil pricing, in many cases Lougheed could not agree to such unfair federal proposals. "If a solution couldn't be negotiated," Premier Davis suggested, "Ottawa should simply impose one. In effect, Davis wanted an emergency declaration that oil is a national resource, not a provincial one. And he was calling for direct federal intervention against the producing provinces" (Braid and Sharpe 1990, 147).

Of course, it wasn't just Ontario politicians demanding Alberta be put in its place. Plenty of other Ontarians wanted that as well. "Newspapers regularly berated the western oil sheiks as un-Canadian. One western journalist, visiting the editorial page editor of the *Toronto Star*, was amazed to hear the man say that Ottawa should send in the troops if Alberta continued to resist" (Braid and Sharpe 1990, 142-143).

Send in the Canadian Army to seize Alberta's oil for Ontario! That was the attitude of a respected Toronto opinion leader.

The Beginning of Alberta Separatism

Premier Peter Lougheed and his government were a strong voice for Alberta, and most Albertans confidently looked to Lougheed to defend the province's interests. This can be seen from Lougheed's three provincial election landslide victories in 1975, 1979, and 1982.

Nevertheless, some Albertans began to conclude that more drastic measures were necessary, so for the first time, organizations supporting Alberta independence began to form in the early 1970s.

According to Professor Roger Gibbins of the University of Calgary, "the best organized and best led of all the western Canadian independence movements" of the 1970s was the Calgary-based Independent Alberta Association (IAA) which formed in 1974.

As Gibbins writes, "Long-standing regional grievances did not provide the immediate impetus to the creation of the IAA; that came from the energy disputes which broke out in the early 70s among the oil industry, Ottawa and the Alberta government" (Gibbins 1980, 189).

This is an important point to keep in mind. Despite frequent conflict between the Prairie West and the federal government going back to the late nineteenth century, it wasn't until the early 1970s that a separatist movement began to organize in the West, particularly in Alberta. This is because it was the policies of Prime Minister Pierre Trudeau, more than any other factor, that was responsible for the rise of Western separatism.

Gibbins quotes IAA president John Rudolph explaining the organization's grievances in a 1974 speech at High River: "the gut issues are the high cost of Confederation, the incredible price we pay to be Albertans, and the rampant spread of socialist philosophy under the guise of every political label possible" (Gibbins 1980, 189).

Rudolph's public speeches gave his organization a certain degree of visibility in Alberta. But there was more to the IAA than that.

> It also commissioned a number of highly publicized reports including the *Cost of Confederation* study by University of Calgary economist Warren Blackman, a study estimating that confederation costs the people of Alberta between one and three billion dollars a year. Yet despite this cost the IAA shied away from advocating independence as a firm goal. Rather the threat of separatism was advanced as a bargaining tool to be used to secure better terms for Alberta and the West within confederation. Only if such terms could not be secured would independence be pursued. To members of the IAA this was a strategy that Quebec had been using effectively for years and one that other regions should be ready and willing to employ (Gibbins 1980, 189).

So it seems that the strategy of saber-rattling to get a better deal for Alberta has been around for almost 50 years. If the IAA were still around today, I think they'd realize that the strategy has failed and the pursuit of outright independence is the only option available to improve Alberta's prospects for the future.

Conclusion

Premier Peter Lougheed fought hard against Pierre Trudeau's government, which was essentially raiding Alberta's oil resources contrary to the constitution. Despite the intensity of that conflict during the 1970s, the worst was yet to come. After the fall of Joe Clark's minority government in December 1979, a re-energized Pierre Trudeau returned to power in February 1980 with a firm agenda to take control of Alberta's oil resources through his National Energy Program.

To this day, many Albertans have not forgotten.

Chapter 2 – The National Energy Program

A federal election was held on May 22, 1979. The Progressive Conservatives under Joe Clark won the most seats, but not enough to form a majority government. As a minority government, Clark tried to reach an energy deal that would find an acceptable compromise between Alberta's desire for higher oil prices and Ontario's desire for low energy prices. That was a goal he could not achieve.

Clark's minister of finance, John Crosbie, introduced a federal budget on December 11, 1979. The budget was opposed by the Liberals and the NDP, so Clark's government was defeated in a vote of confidence on December 13, 1979. Therefore, another federal election was scheduled for February 18, 1980.

The 1980 federal election was very significant for Alberta. As University of Regina sociologist John Conway wrote, that "election, and its aftermath, sparked the most serious confrontation between the West and Ottawa in the twentieth century" (Conway 2014, 173).

The most controversial aspect of Crosbie's budget was an 18-cent per gallon tax increase on gasoline. Many Canadians did not want to pay that much more for gas. Canadians – especially in the eastern provinces – wanted lower energy prices, not higher. This made Alberta's desire to receive a fair price for its oil controversial in other parts of the country.

> The West was seriously isolated, since all other regions wanted lower energy prices than the West wanted. The rest of Canada generally supported federal initiatives to regulate energy prices and to capture a share of the boom from Western energy exports to help off-set the spiraling costs of energy in the consuming provinces. The West's complaints received less and less sympathy in the rest of Canada (Conway 2014, 174).

Indeed, "many Central and Atlantic Canadians saw the demands of the West as motivated by greed and sectionalism" (Conway 2014, 174).

The media stoked the negative messaging about Alberta. "An exaggerated view of the booming West was purveyed by the Central and Atlantic Canadian press and politicians, rendering the West's complaints unconvincing to most Canadians. The headlines, while based on fact, created an image of a rich, arrogant, and selfish West" (Conway 2014, 174-175).

Of course, this was exactly the same message as Trudeau's Liberals were propagating. The Liberals deliberately promoted an extremely divisive anti-West message as a way to generate support in Central Canada and thereby get back into power.

> During the election campaign in February 1980, the Liberals had fanned resentment of the West in order to gain votes in Central Canada. Candidates repeatedly

told audiences, much as they had in the 1970s, that the oil and gas producing provinces were being selfish; that they didn't want to share their new-found wealth; that it was unfair for excess wealth to build up in less populated areas of the country (Nemeth 2006, 692-693).

With that sort of image being portrayed in much of the country, Trudeau was seen as the man who could put Alberta in its place – subordinate to Central Canadian interests.

It was therefore not surprising that Trudeau was re-elected with a majority government in the February 1980 election. There is no doubt that the victory can be largely attributed to Trudeau's promise to Central and Atlantic Canadians that he would keep the lid on the West's demands for increased oil prices and that he would continue to frustrate Western efforts to gain unimpeded jurisdiction over resources, especially energy resources (Conway 2014, 176-177).

In short, Trudeau would keep Alberta under his foot. "For this, the Ontario electorate rewarded him" (Conway 2014, 177).

When the National Energy Program (NEP) was introduced in October 1980, it "was seen as Ontario's reward for helping to re-elect the Liberals" (Braid and Sharpe 1990, 150).

The purpose of the NEP was to put an end to the growing economic and political clout of the West, especially Alberta. "This program unilaterally imposed federal authority over energy resources and established new price and revenue sharing regimes in the absence of consent from the West" (Conway 2014, 177).

Never before – or since – has the federal government targeted a particular province for ruin the way Pierre Trudeau's government went after Alberta with the NEP.

Trudeau and his people were aware of the negative response they were going to receive from Westerners. Before the NEP was released, Deputy Minister of Finance Ian Stewart wrote that

> the energy proposals as they now stand, would be seen by many to be the biggest revenue grab in the history of the country. EMR's [Energy, Mines and Resources] tax and pricing measures would allow eastern oil and gas consumers to continue enjoying massive rents (via lower prices) and the federal treasury to collect billions from a gas export tax, both of which would reinforce western alienation (Nemeth 2006, 684).

The Liberal's Minister of Energy, Mines and Resources at the time was Marc Lalonde. He met with some Alberta officials to give the appearance of working with the province in developing the new energy policy. But "Lalonde, and his officials, had no intention of seriously negotiating with Alberta and planned from the start to impose an energy package unilaterally" (Nemeth 2006, 685).

When the NEP was announced in October 1980, the policy document stated that "one provincial government – not all, and not the national government – enjoys most of the windfall, under current policies. These policies are no longer compatible with the national interest" (Nemeth 2006, 686).

Since 1973, oil produced in Canada had been priced well below world prices for the benefit of Central Canada, and the NEP made that policy permanent.

In 1973, the Canadian well-head price was C$3.66 a barrel while the world price was C$10.50 a barrel; in 1980, the Canadian well-head price was C$16.75 a barrel while the world price was C$44.66. Moreover, prices under the NEP were unilaterally imposed, rather than negotiated, and specified that the maximum price for conventional crude would never go beyond 85 percent of the world price. In other words, controlled prices had become a permanent rather than a temporary policy (Nemeth 2006, 687).

It's very important to understand who benefited from this policy. Alberta's oil exports "were sold at the world price, but the federal government took the difference between the Canadian and the export price through the Oil Export Charge. The rationale for this was to help reduce consumer costs of the imported oil that was still entering Eastern Canada at world prices" (Nemeth 2006, 687).

Soon after the NEP was announced, Premier Lougheed indicated – on television – that Alberta's response would be to cutback oil production.

Soon after Lougheed's televised address in response to the NEP, Marc Lalonde compared Alberta to Quebec separatists. He then polarized East and West by adding a consumer tax to pay for increased oil imports caused by the Alberta production cutbacks, which he called the "Lougheed Levy." If consumers wanted to know who was responsible for higher prices at the pumps, Lalonde wanted to be sure they would think that it was Alberta (Nemeth 2006, 693).

The cutbacks forced Trudeau to negotiate with Alberta, and a revenue sharing agreement was reached between Trudeau and Lougheed in September 1981 – although not to the satisfaction of many Albertans.

Then, in 1984, Brian Mulroney's Tories beat the Liberals in a federal election and began to dismantle the NEP.

Dr. Tammy Nemeth's analysis is absolutely correct: "The NEP was a turning point for Alberta. Never before had a federal government attempted such a comprehensive restructuring of the federal-provincial balance of power and of an industry predominantly located in one province" (Nemeth 2006, 696).

When the NEP was announced, the federal government said it was needed to achieve Canadian energy self-sufficiency, Canadianize the oil industry by reducing American ownership, and to provide fair energy prices for Canadians.

Years after he left office, however, former Energy Minister Marc Lalonde admitted to journalist Ron Graham that those weren't the real reasons for implementing the NEP. Instead, Lalonde said,

> The major factor behind the NEP wasn't Canadianization or getting more from the industry or even self-sufficiency. *The* determinant factor was the fiscal imbalance between the provinces and the federal government in the scenario in which the provincial revenues would go up with the price of oil while Ottawa's share of the larger and larger pie got smaller and smaller.... Our proposal was to increase Ottawa's share appreciably, so that the share of the producing provinces would decline significantly and the industry's share would decline somewhat (Graham 1987, 81).

In other words, the actual goal of the NEP was to reduce Alberta's share of revenue from its own resources, while dramatically increasing the federal government's take. It's almost like the Trudeau government was unilaterally turning back the clock to before 1930, when the federal government owned Alberta's resources.

The NEP appeared to be a form of economic war on Alberta.

Indeed, it was so unfair that even Prime Minister Brian Mulroney later acknowledged how bad it was. He told journalists Don Braid and Sydney Sharpe that "the National Energy Program is exactly like a hold-up at a gas station at three in the morning. That's what they did! No one with a brain in his head is placing in doubt the fact that the Liberal government went in and knowingly pillaged the economy of Alberta'" (Braid and Sharpe 1990, 162).

"Pillage" is a good word to describe the real goal of the NEP, as admitted by Lalonde above.

The Effect of the NEP

It's no exaggeration to say that Alberta was hit hard by the NEP.

> It has been stated that by September 1983 the number of oil rigs operating in Alberta dropped from 400 to 130 and that upwards of $70 billion was lost to the Alberta economy in the first few years of the NEP. To put this in context, American producing states like Texas, Oklahoma, Alaska and Louisiana experienced a significant economic boom from 1980 until prices started to soften in 1983 and collapsed in 1986. Most scholars agree that the sharp downturn in Alberta's economy, unlike Texas and other oil producing

American states, occurred before the oil prices collapsed and was a direct result of the NEP (Nemeth 2006, 691).

Thousands of jobs were lost and countless businesses went under. Without question, the NEP damaged Alberta significantly.

Two distinguished economists, Mike Percy of the University of Alberta and Robert Mansell of the University of Calgary, concluded that "the NEP was the crucial factor that kicked Alberta into deep recession in 1982, primarily because it pulled out money and killed investment at the same time" (Braid and Sharpe 1990, 186).

So far, the main emphasis of this book has been on the energy wars between Alberta and Ottawa in the 1970s, culminating in the National Energy Program in the early 1980s. In 1991, *Alberta Report* founder Ted Byfield wrote a very effective summary of this period, and it's especially worth reading to get his perspective on the situation.

Byfield's emphasis is on how Pierre Trudeau's government decided to change the rules governing Canada in order to benefit Ontario and Quebec at Alberta's expense:

> First it applied an export tax on oil—Canada had never before charged an export tax on anything—neatly siphoning off the added revenue to the federal treasury, and using the revenues to reduce the price of oil in Toronto and Montreal.
>
> Then in 1980 the Trudeau government won election, with the full support of the Conservative government of Ontario, by promising to impose federal taxes directly on Alberta resources. This, of course, was

against the law. But how do you "arrest" the federal government? The tax men entered the oil company offices and applied the taxes. Were these companies supposed to bar the doors? They had no option but to pay.

So the rules of the Canada game were now to be changed. They were sacrosanct only so long as Ontario and Quebec won by them. If the game started to go badly, you changed the rules. Alberta must learn to "share" with the rest of Canada, said Trudeau's energy minister, Marc Lalonde. Well, therefore, would a federal tax be levied on Quebec Hydro exports? Would Quebec be required to "share" its electric power with Nova Scotia, which depended on oil-fueled thermal generators? Well no, that was a very different matter.

More and more it began to look as though Canada was a mere con game, being played out by Ontario and Quebec at the expense of the West. And the numbers proved it. Between 1969 and 1984, Alberta transferred more than $95 billion to the rest of Canada, most of it to Quebec, which gained $80 billion out of tax transfers and energy benefits during the same period. This money, had it remained in Alberta, would have financed industrial diversification in the bust that followed. But by then the money was gone (Byfield 1991, 3).

Byfield makes the point strikingly clear. Yes, when it came to the energy wars, Canada was a "mere con game, being played out by Ontario and Quebec at the expense of the West."

Albertans should keep this in mind because not much has changed.

Conclusion

From 1973 onward, Alberta's energy resources were being pillaged by Pierre Trudeau's government with the support of Central Canada. Albertans tend to be patriotic Canadians, but eventually the abuse was too much. When the Western Canada Concept Party of Alberta (WCC) was formed in 1981, Albertans had a new vehicle with which to fight back.

The WCC won a by-election in 1982, and one of its most prominent members led an important campaign against Trudeau's proposed *Charter of Rights and Freedoms*. Ominously, the Charter deliberately omitted property rights, and this defect will never be rectified.

Chapter 3 - The Western Canada Concept Party of Alberta

Although there had been organizations advocating Alberta independence during the 1970s, support for that option did not become widely popular until Pierre Trudeau was re-elected in February 1980, after the short-lived Joe Clark minority government. Support for independence subsequently exploded when the Trudeau government announced its devastating National Energy Program (NEP) in October 1980. Several large independence meetings were held in the aftermath of that announcement—at least one with more than two thousand people.

Over time, the meetings became smaller and less frequent. But subsequent events – namely, a by-election – would demonstrate that support for independence had not faded away.

Most by-elections are not particularly important. They usually occur to fill a seat in the legislature or parliament between general elections, often due to the resignation of the sitting member. Frequently, the opposition party will pick up the seat, indicating dissatisfaction with the governing party, but rarely does the outcome have much effect.

In certain cases, however, a by-election can have huge symbolic significance. This was the case in 1982, when Gordon Kesler won a by-election in the Olds-Didsbury riding for the Western Canada Concept Party of Alberta (WCC). Kesler's victory was like a shot heard across the country. It was the first time a member of a separatist party was ever elected in Western Canada. Clearly, many Albertans were extremely concerned about the threat posed by Pierre Trudeau's federal government and were willing to consider new alternatives.

In 1981, the Alberta independence movement was dominated by two rival organizations: a non-party association called West-Fed, and a brand-new political party, the aforementioned WCC. However, in the course of that year, support for both groups began to cool off and some observers believed that the independence movement had already peaked. "At times it seemed that the movement was dying" (Ray 1984, 159).

During 1981, major internal problems became evident within the independence movement, especially involving leadership squabbles. "This issue of leadership credibility bedeviled both organizations. The West-Fed of Calgary had three changes in leadership between September 1980 and December 1981. The fourth group of leaders went over to the WCC in December, which had also been having its own problems" (Ray 1984, 161).

As a result, the independence movement essentially discredited itself in the eyes of the public. The mass support evident in late 1980 seemed to fade away, and both organizations lost much of their public profile. It looked like excitement over independence had been just a flash-in-the-pan.

Because the movement was at such a low point, commentators "dismissed western separatism as being dead, burnt-out" (Ray 1984, 161).

But they were in for a surprise. "On Wednesday, February 17, 1982, Gordon Kesler took western separatism out of the museum of Canadian oddities and planted the WCC banner on the ramparts of a shocked Canada" (Ray 1984, 161).

On November 30, 1981, former Alberta Social Credit Party leader and MLA for Olds-Didsbury, Bob Clark, resigned his seat in the legislature. This created a vacancy requiring a by-election. The territory within that riding had been held by the Social Credit Party for most of the 46 years since William Aberhart's stunning election victory of 1935. However, Social Credit had been in decline for at least ten years, and Peter Lougheed's Progressive Conservatives dominated Alberta politics.

The WCC chose Gordon Kesler as its candidate for the impending by-election.

> Kesler owned his own oil scouting firm, was involved in farming and had been a rodeo cowboy since the age of eight. The WCC used his background shrewdly, showing Kesler as having his feet planted in both agriculture and oil. They also displayed him as a religious man (part of the WCC's programme was a belief in God) (Ray 1984, 163).

The upstart WCC was not expected to win. In contrast to that party, both the Tories and Socreds had strong organizations in the riding.

> The victory was all the more remarkable because the WCC was only two years old and had been registered in Alberta for only eight months. Its organized constituency association in Olds-Didsbury was less than seven months old at the time of the election call. In only four weeks the Olds-Didsbury WCC grew from barely forty-five members to be the winning party. Kesler was given 4,015 votes, representing 42.16 percent of the vote (Ray 1984, 162).

The impact of Kesler's victory was very significant. For one, it led to a consolidation of the independence movement behind the WCC. West-Fed disbanded and recommended that its members join the WCC.

> The benefits of the by-election victory were hard to miss. [A]fter Olds-Didsbury the separatist movement in Alberta emerged for a short while as a consolidated force, with a sense of vitality and an expectation that perhaps it could win the provincial government. In the month after the WCC victory, even Tory sources were conceding as many as twenty seats to the WCC in the next election. Before Olds-Didsbury, voting for a separatist party was not publicly acceptable behaviour. . . . The WCC had been catapulted to national prominence (Ray 1984, 166).

After the by-election, membership in the party grew rapidly. However, the party once again descended into leadership conflicts and in-house squabbling.

Faced with a party that was both growing as a threat but also mired by internal strife, Premier Lougheed smartly called an early provincial election for November. The Tories won 75 of 79 seats, with the NDP picking up 2, and the remaining 2 going to independents who previously had been Social Credit MLAs.

The WCC was shut-out despite receiving 11.76 per cent of the provincial vote. This was a heavy loss.

Viewed from another angle, the WCC results were impressive. Just over two years of organizing in Alberta had resulted in registered constituency associations in all but one riding and nearly twelve percent of the popular vote. If seats had been allocated on the basis of popular vote, the WCC would have won nine seats! The WCC emerged from the election with a province-wide, battle-tested organization and a substantial popular base (Ray 1984, 168).

The subsequent history of the Alberta WCC is largely one of decline, and most of its supporters would later be absorbed by the Reform Party of Canada.

However, its brief moment in the sun is worth remembering as the time an Alberta riding sent Pierre Trudeau a resounding message he would never forget. The Olds-Didsbury by-election had a national impact and gave the idea of Alberta independence a degree of credibility for the first time.

When a Republican president inspired Alberta patriots

The by-election victory was unquestionably the most important event in building credibility for Alberta's independence movement. But there were other factors that helped to lend it additional credibility.

For example, the election of President Ronald Reagan in 1980 conferred considerable new prominence and credibility on conservative ideas not only in the United States, but in

Western Canada as well. This bolstered the case for the free enterprise ideals that were championed by Alberta separatists.

As mentioned, the Alberta independence movement began to take shape in the 1970s and really took off after the re-election of Pierre Trudeau in February 1980. It was well-understood at the time that independence supporters were ideologically small-c conservatives. After all, a major component of the conflict with Trudeau was whether Canada's energy needs were best served by free enterprise (i.e., the oilmen who actually built the petroleum industry) or socialistic policies (i.e., federal government central planners in Ottawa). Small-c conservatives, of course, clearly favoured the first alternative, whereas leftists (whether Red Tories, Liberals or New Democrats) favoured the second.

The decades after the Great Depression saw free enterprise ideals lose ground to the ideals of government planning. Keynesian economics became popular, and governments in Western countries foolishly believed they could manipulate the economy to create prosperity. Pierre Trudeau's execrable NEP fell within this stream of thought. In fact, free market economics was so out-of-style that in 1980 Memorial University sociologist J. D. House published his study of Calgary oilmen under the title, *The Last of the Free Enterprisers*.

With this in mind, the significance of Reagan's election for the Alberta independence movement can be understood. As University of Calgary political scientist Roger Gibbins wrote, "the Reaganite drift, if not stampede, to neoconservatism offers moral support to the separatists' ideological crusade" (Gibbins 1981, 206).

That is to say, the election of Ronald Reagan provided a degree of credibility for the conservative political ideals of Alberta's independence supporters that had not existed previously.

The ideological perspective of the independence movement was essentially the same as American conservativism and Reagan's success strengthened the movement's legitimacy. As Gibbins explained,
> This correspondence with the United States provides considerable moral support for the separatist cause for it appears to place the separatists within the mainstream of contemporary North American political thought. Even though the ideological position of the separatists is a minority one within Canada, even though the separatist supporters have been the ideological losers in a wide range of policy decisions over the past few decades, the American scene holds out the promise that the separatists are riding the ideological wave of the future rather than of the past (Gibbins 1981, 203-204).

In other words, independence supporters were no longer political "dinosaurs" resisting the inevitable tide of history towards socialism. Instead, they were part of a broader trend towards limited government that had taken hold in the world's largest and most powerful country. The election of Ronald Reagan clearly indicated that the oilmen of Calgary weren't "the last of the free enterprisers" after all.

Political conservatism was not the only point of ideological convergence between Westerners and Americans. As Gibbins noted,

In the past, the ideological climates of the Canadian and American Wests shared a populist base; political protest in both regions arrayed "the people" against the established political institutions rooted in central Canada and the eastern seaboard of the United States. Populism is still characteristic of the separatist movement and in that sense serves to entwine the separatist movement with American political values. In the United States populism has not been subordinated to the confining practices of parliamentary democracy, and it continues to play a vibrant role in the political culture. Thus the separatists' deep suspicion of representative democracy, the charge that the West is subjected to taxation without representation, the muted call for a tax revolt, and the West-Fed proposal for a popularly elected constituent assembly are all more in keeping with the populist thought that spread north into Canada in the early decades of this century, and which still vitalizes American politics, than they are with Canadian political experience and traditions (Gibbins 1981, 205-206).

Populism is commonly believed to have been a major factor in the election of President Donald Trump in 2016, and populism is still evident in Alberta's political culture.

The general similarity of political perspectives between people in the Canadian West and the U.S. did not go unnoticed, especially among supporters of Alberta independence. As Gibbins explained,

To separatists, the West is not only different from the East but is also very similar to the United States in terms of political values and ideological predispositions; the West is placed within the mainstream of American, although not Canadian, values. This correspondence, it should be noted, is widely assumed by western Canadians. In its October 1980 survey of 1230 western Canadian respondents the Canada West Foundation found that fifty-three per cent agreed, and only thirty-six percent disagreed, with the statement that "in many ways western Canadians have more in common with the western United States than with eastern Canada" (Gibbins 1981, 204).

There are certain historical parallels between the early 1980s and the period of the Donald Trump presidency (2017-2021): Trudeau prime ministers in Canada and controversial Republican presidents in the United States. The ideological movements undergirding both presidents provided a degree of ideological credibility to Alberta's independence supporters – conservatism in the case of President Reagan and populism in the case of President Trump.

The Alberta independence movement arose in the early 1980s – and came back to life after the 2015 federal election – due to domestic events, not foreign ones. Nevertheless, it is not uncommon for political movements of both the left and right in Canada to be inspired by events in the United States (Black Lives Matter and "gay pride" events being conspicuous recent examples on the left). In this vein, the conservative success represented by the election of President Reagan provided credibility to the ideological perspective of Alberta's independence movement in the 1980s.

Alberta's Woman of the Century vs. Pierre Trudeau's 1982 Constitution

Another factor contributing to the credibility of the Alberta independence movement was the participation of a couple of important thinkers.

During the first big wave of the Alberta independence movement in the early 1980s, the most prominent intellectuals involved were Prof. Warren Blackman of the University of Calgary, and Dr. Ruth Gorman, a civil rights lawyer. Prof. Blackman was an economist who believed that Western Canada would flourish as an independent country. Dr. Gorman was more concerned that Prime Minister Pierre Trudeau's new constitution would erode our rights and freedoms.

The outrage felt in Alberta due to Trudeau's NEP has already been discussed. His socialistic ambitions with that policy were clear.

But he also had another major initiative at the same time – to repatriate Canada's constitution from Britain and add to it his so-called *Charter of Rights and Freedoms*. It was this constitutional agenda, more than anything else, that fueled Ruth Gorman's opposition to Trudeau and his government.

What's particularly interesting is that Gorman was best known as an early feminist and a champion of the rights of First Nations people. She was one of only two women to graduate with law degrees from the University of Alberta in 1939. Later, she became a leading activist defending the treaty rights of Aboriginal Canadians, and helped them gain voting rights in 1960.

Gorman received an honorary doctorate from the University of Calgary in 1966, and was named Alberta Woman of the Century in 1967.

Despite her activism, Frits Pannekoek of Athabasca University writes that Gorman "was a Conservative and populist" (Pannekoek 2007, xlii). She was a friend of Prime Minister John Diefenbaker and a supporter of his government.

When Pierre Trudeau initiated repatriation of the constitution, Gorman helped found the Western Canada Concept Party of Alberta. According to Pannekoek, "she became involved with the political party with a passion. She developed its constitution and did much of its legal work" (Pannekoek 2007, xxvi).

Gorman gave speeches and wrote articles against Trudeau's proposed constitution. In one 1981 speech, she called it "the most serious threat to our individual freedoms and our financial future that we have ever been called upon to face" (Gorman n.d., 1).

Her main concern with the new constitution was the absence of property rights. The single biggest flaw, she explained, "is your loss of property rights. For 900 years, since Magna Charta which said 'Every individual must be permanently secured in the free enjoyment of his life and property' you have had this right. Now the guarantee for the individuals' or the provinces' property rights has been deliberately omitted from Canada's new constitution" (Gorman n.d., 1).

The wealth of Western Canada is rooted in its land and resources. The pioneers came to the West to get land and to own property for themselves. By the 1970s, the West's resources were really beginning to pay off, but Gorman argued that Trudeau's constitution posed a genuine threat to this prosperity:

> The removal of property rights was deliberate. It is to legalize the robbery slowly and whenever necessary of the West's only proven great asset to date, our property. This now is to be taken to assure the perpetuation of

power for the central government at Ottawa, taken to pay Ottawa's vast debts and to buy the votes to keep them in power (Gorman n.d., 2-3).

In a February 3, 1981, column for the *Calgary Herald*, Gorman wrote that "Most countries lose these rights when tanks rumble across their borders; you are losing yours by a few pages of print" (Gorman 1981).

Of course, by that time many Albertans were outraged at Trudeau and were attending meetings held by pro-independence groups. As Gorman explained,
> The threat of becoming central Canada's colony is causing protest meetings across the West already, and forcing people to think about the alternative of independence. Our ancestors came to this country because it was free. Our fathers, brothers, and sons fought for that freedom in two wars, and many died. Westerners now must make another stand for their freedoms. And you must do it now (Gorman 1981).

Of course, the protest meetings came to an end and Trudeau got his repatriated constitution and his so-called *Charter of Rights*. But most people today have forgotten that in the early 1980s there was strong opposition to Trudeau's *Charter* from many Canadians, especially in the West. Manitoba premier Sterling Lyon is particularly noteworthy in this regard. Those who think that Pierre Trudeau gave us our individual rights with his Charter need a history lesson.

Despite the passage of time, Ruth Gorman's words continue to resonate today. Westerners "must make another stand for their freedoms," and they need to do it now.

Lack of property rights in the Charter

Ruth Gorman was right about the threat to property rights posed by Pierre Trudeau's *Charter of Rights*.

In the historic Anglo-American tradition, the purpose of a constitutionally-entrenched individual rights document is to protect citizens from their own government. Seventeenth century English political theorist John Locke famously summarized these protections as the rights to life, liberty, and property. The government can't kill, imprison, or confiscate the possessions of its citizens without legitimate justification (e.g., citizens who are violent criminals).

Canada's *Charter of Rights and Freedoms*, adopted in 1982 after great effort by Prime Minister Pierre Trudeau, essentially followed in this historic tradition. That is why it was an easy sell to Canadians in the early 1980s. Supposedly, the *Charter* would protect us from the government. Who doesn't want that?

However, opponents of the *Charter* at that time – which included many Albertans – were very concerned about its deliberate failure to include property rights, one of the three key protections listed by Locke. By not including property rights, Canada's Charter deviated from the historic Anglo-American heritage. This signaled that the Charter would not protect individual rights in the same way, or to the same degree, as previous rights documents.

In 2015, University of Saskatchewan law professor Dwight Newman and his research assistant, Lorelle Binnion, wrote an article for the *Alberta Law Review* to explain why property rights were deliberately left out.

As the Charter was being drafted in the early 1980s, there was support for property rights from many citizens as well as the federal Progressive Conservative Party. Influential organizations, such as the Business Council on National Issues and the Canadian Bar Association, also supported them.

However, the New Democratic Party was strongly opposed to property rights, and would not support Trudeau's proposals unless they were excluded. So, in short, Trudeau catered to the NDP's demands to get that party's support. As Newman and Binnion put it, "Property rights were sacrificed so the rest of the *Charter* and the Constitution could move forward, making apparent that property rights had not been central to Trudeau's vision of the *Charter* even if he would have supported them" (Newman and Binnion 2015, 556).

They point out that Trudeau was willing to bargain away property rights, "something he would not have done with other rights provisions" (Newman and Binnion 2015, 558). Unsurprisingly, with his leftist ideological bent, Pierre Trudeau had no qualms about entrenching a document that excluded property rights.

Newman and Binnion point out that property rights were omitted to satisfy a small ideological element that punched far above its weight: "Those who opposed property rights outright — some of them on full-fledged ideological grounds, because of favouring social ownership of the means of production — achieved an impact far beyond their numbers in achieving the exclusion of property rights" (Newman and Binnion 2015, 558).

In short, property rights were sacrificed as a direct result of socialist influence in writing the Charter.

There were two main results from this. First, and most obviously, protections for property rights in Canada are much weaker than protections for other basic rights. On top of that, the exclusion of property rights signaled to judges that restrictions on government power are not as extensive as they are in other Anglo-American jurisdictions. Some jurisdictions protect the historic rights of life, liberty, and property. But Canada's protects life, liberty, and ... well, that's it. The restrictions on government power are less by conscious design.

The NDP, with Trudeau's complete concurrence, did not want government power restricted too much. How could socialism be implemented in Canada if citizens had constitutionally-entrenched property rights? That would be a socialist's nightmare. The socialist vision of a New Society cannot be imposed by governments if individuals have too much power vis-à-vis the state. In other words, the ideological message communicated by the deliberate exclusion of property rights is that the Charter's limitations on government power only go so far.

As Newman and Binnion explain,
Had the *Charter* contained the full set of classical rights, including property rights, the holistic reading of the *Charter* would presumably have been different, or at least ought to have been. On such a revised holistic reading, the presence of the property rights provision could have led to other rights being read differently (Newman and Binnion 2015, 563).

In other words, "the text and symbolism of a *Charter* without property rights has led to a different overall interpretation of the *Charter* compared to a text with property rights" (Newman and Binnion 2015, 564).

The exclusion of property rights communicates that Canada's Charter is unlike other rights documents in the historic Anglo-American tradition. In contrast to the U.S. Bill of Rights, for example, Canada's Charter had direct socialist influence on its drafting, so its protection of individual rights is thereby reduced. Therefore, Canadians should not be surprised when judges rule that infringements on their liberties are justified under the Charter.

Conclusion

Trudeau's NEP led to considerable anger in Alberta, resulting in some political success for the WCC, notably a by-election victory. But another aspect of the WCC was its opposition to Trudeau's constitutional agenda, best represented in the work of Dr. Ruth Gorman. Her perspective continues to be relevant because the *Charter of Rights* as adopted deliberately omitted property rights. This is still the situation today, and all Canadians have less constitutional protections as a result.

As will next be discussed, most Albertans have believed that the province's problems could be solved either by replacing the governing party or reforming the constitution. Thus the 1984 election of Brian Mulroney's Progressive Conservative government was widely welcomed by Albertans. Unfortunately, most Albertans would become disappointed by Mulroney and the province's difficulties within Canada remained largely unaddressed.

Also, a major effort to reform the constitution – by adopting a Triple-E Senate – was launched from Alberta. This, too, failed to solve the province's problems.

Making political or constitutional changes to improve Alberta's lot within Canada were sensible and noble courses of action. But the failure of those initiatives clearly demonstrates that attempting to reform Canada is a dead end. Only the pursuit of independence can result in Alberta having control of its own future to achieve freedom and prosperity.

Chapter 4 – The Alternatives Have Failed

Picture this: a Liberal federal government beating up on Alberta. Albertans looking to the Conservative Party to rescue them from their Liberal tormentors. A federal election leading to a Conservative victory, with every seat in Alberta choosing a Conservative MP.

Doesn't this sound like the hope of many Albertans today? Yet the situation being described is the early 1980s. Pierre Trudeau – that arch-enemy of Alberta – resigned in 1984, and later that year the Liberal government was replaced by Brian Mulroney's Progressive Conservatives.

It looked like Alberta's problems were over. The hated Liberals were out of power and could harm the province no longer. Brian Mulroney was the West's saviour and would make things right.

But wait. Something went wrong. Less than 3 years later, the Reform Association of Canada voted to create a new political party to represent the West. In 1993, that new political party – the Reform Party of Canada – blew the federal Conservatives out of the West. The West's saviour of 1984 had betrayed his Western supporters.

It couldn't happen again, right? The Conservatives have learned their lesson. They won't let the West down this time.

Don't be so sure. The same factors that turned Brian Mulroney from a saviour into a villain are still dominating Canadian politics. Any party wishing to form government must win most of the federal seats in Ontario and/or Quebec. Thus, advancing the interests of those two provinces over the interests of the West will always be the policy of Canada's federal government.

The Hope of 1984

To Albertans, the 1984 federal election represented the height of success: all the provinces 21 MPs were Progressive Conservative and therefore part of the government caucus. Some of them even became cabinet ministers. Clearly, the federal government would be on Alberta's side, right?

Lethbridge College political scientist Faron Ellis has described the situation this way:

> For many western Canadians the 1984 Progressive Conservative victory represented a watershed. After decades of witnessing the majority of their federal representatives relegated to opposition status, most westerners believed they would finally see their concerns seriously addressed by a federal government within which they now had substantial representation. The prevailing view was that western MPs, sitting in cabinet and the government caucus, would now have the power to redress the large number of regional grievances resulting from successive Liberal governments preoccupied with central Canadian

concerns in general, and Quebec concerns in particular. By changing the players, it was thought, the current party and electoral system would finally work to the advantage of western Canadians. This attitude, while prevalent across the West, was centred in Alberta and dominated the political culture of that province. Thus, it was in Alberta where levels of western alienation were highest and where expectations of redress were strongest (Ellis 2005, 17-18).

Yet, as he goes on to explain, the expected redress was not to occur. "Although western MPs held more seats in the first Mulroney cabinet than westerners had ever held before, and many were senior cabinet portfolios, almost immediately, western interests again seemed to take a back seat to Central interests" (Ellis 2005, 18).

University of Calgary political scientist Roger Gibbins describes the outcome of the 1984 election in similar terms:
One prime minister from Quebec – Pierre Trudeau – had been replaced by another prime minister from Quebec – Brian Mulroney – with the two individuals differing at the margins if at all in their orientations toward Quebec, bilingualism, and the basic parameters of the Canadian federal state and political community (Gibbins 1988, 338).

From this perspective, despite what Albertans expected, the 1984 election didn't really usher in significant change at all.

As Gibbins explains, the Liberal caucus of the early 1980s had 74 MPs from Quebec who ensured that the government would be very sensitive to Quebec's concerns. And the first term of the Mulroney administration also had a sizable contingent of Quebec MPs – 58 – that had a major influence on government policy.

So while the governing party changed in 1984, the dominating influence of Quebec did not:
> In this case, then, the orientation of the national government to Quebec and Quebec-related issues was not changed by the 1984 election. The fundamental transformation has occurred instead *within* the Progressive Conservative party, which for the first time since 1958 has a sizable contingent of Quebec MPs, and which for the first time ever has a Quebec leader (Gibbins 1988, 338).

The PC party became the dominant federal party of the West beginning in 1958, due to the leadership of Saskatchewan populist, John Diefenbaker. From that point forward, the West constituted the heartland of the PC party.

But as Gibbins notes, the election of large numbers of Tory MPs from central Canada in 1984 meant that the West would take a back seat in the party's priorities. "In the four federal elections held between 1972 and 1980, western Canadian MPs constituted 44 percent of the federal Tory caucus, while following the 1984 election this proportion dropped to only 27 percent" (Gibbins 1988, 347).

Even though the West had finally achieved a milestone in electing MPs into government, it simultaneously "lost the Conservatives as a regional champion" (Gibbins 1988, 347).

Ellis describes what happened next:
> Westerners seemingly watched from the sidelines again as the Conservatives were slow in dismantling the National Energy Program and made little headway in

reducing government spending and the federal deficit. Meanwhile, the Conservatives moved to position themselves within the issue space of the former Liberal government by continuing to accommodate the demands of many left-of-centre interest groups, by promoting bilingualism, and making no recognizable progress on criminal justice reform. The government also embarked on a monetary policy directed at cooling the overheated central Canadian economy while the West headed deeper into recession. A flashpoint occurred in the fall of 1986 when the federal cabinet decided to award Montreal's Canadair with a substantial military contract to maintain Canada's CF-18 fleet despite a technically and financially superior bid from Winnipeg's Bristol Aerospace. It was at this time, only two years into the first Mulroney mandate, that a small group of westerners began organizing another formal political protest against the established parties (Ellis 2005, 18-19).

Awarding the CF-18 contract to Quebec despite the fact that Manitoba won it under the government's own criteria was an absolute outrage. This was an obvious example of the federal government catering to central Canada at the expense of the West. The "organizing" that Ellis refers to led to the creation of the Reform Party of Canada.

The point is, though, that a federal government can only be elected when a party wins a large proportion of the seats in central Canada. Since the majority of voters and seats are in Ontario and Quebec, the federal government will always favour those two provinces. It can't be any other way and the CF-18 incident revealed that in spades.

Current Conservative Party of Canada leader Pierre Poilievre – like every other leader – must satisfy the voters of central Canada if he wants to become prime minister. If he were to win, a substantial portion of his caucus will be from central Canada and he will owe his position to them.

This is how the system works.

Even someone as favourable to the West as Prime Minister Stephen Harper was severely constrained in what he could accomplish due to the basic logic of the system.

Undoubtedly, Poilievre would be a much better prime minister than Justin Trudeau. His policies would be likely beneficial for Alberta. But at best he would be a reprieve until the next Liberal government is elected and Alberta once again comes under attack from the federal government.

A Prime Minister Poilievre could not fix Canada's political system in a way that would improve Alberta's situation. Central Canada would not allow it, and that's where power lies. Indeed, Poilievre is MP for an Ontario riding and he will prioritize Ontario ahead of Alberta. It's only right that an MP puts the interests of his own constituents first.

Only by becoming independent would Alberta be able to elect leaders who would put Albertans' interests first. That's the bottom line.

The Reform Party of Canada

As mentioned above, the CF-18 affair sparked the creation of the Reform Party of Canada. When the CF-18 contract was awarded to Quebec, Ted Byfield writes, "Albertans recognized the symptoms. It didn't matter which party was in power at Ottawa. Unless the rules were changed, the West would be exploited permanently" (Byfield 1991, 4).

Thus, the Reform Party of Canada began forming under the leadership of Preston Manning. Manning wanted the new party to advocate for the West getting equal treatment within Canada rather than separating from Canada. As Byfield relates it,

> No longer would the West talk about "getting out of Canada." Instead the slogan became, "The West Wants In," a phrase coined by *Alberta Report* columnist Ralph Hedlin. It means that the West wants constitutional changes that will enable it to play a more equal role in Canadian affairs, notably a Triple-E Senate (Byfield 1991, 5).

The precursor organization to the Reform Party was the Reform Association of Canada. Members of the association decided to form a new party in 1987. A brochure was then produced explaining the basis of the new party, and it described the political situation faced by the West:

> Throughout our history, Ontario and Quebec have held the lion's share of political influence in Canada, and they continue to dominate the national scene at the expense of the West.
>
> Our political and economic development is being hamstrung by the vested interests of the "Golden Triangle" establishment of Toronto – Ottawa – Montreal.
>
> The massive $65 billion raid on the Alberta economy perpetrated by the Trudeau Liberals through their National Energy Program is a good example of how Western economic development has been frustrated.
>
> More recently, the Mulroney government's award of a $1.4 billion CF-18 aircraft maintenance contract to

Canadair of Montreal, despite a significantly lower bid by the technologically superior Bristol Aerospace of Winnipeg, has shown how politically entrenched this eastern bias is.

In the last federal election, Westerners voted overwhelmingly in favour of the Progressive Conservative Party, because they firmly believed in the Mulroney promise of a "new era" in relations between Ottawa and the West.

This "new era" has not developed. The Western economy continues to languish and Western influence in national economic and political decision making is insufficient to bring about meaningful change (Reform Association of Canada 1987).

This statement is particularly interesting because, aside from a few historical details, it still accurately describes the situation today despite being written 36 years ago. Although the Reform Party had considerable electoral success in the West, nothing has really changed in terms of the West's mistreatment within Canada.

The Triple-E Senate

To a large degree, the Reform Party saw Senate reform as the indispensable way to improve the West's situation within Canada.

The reasoning for this position was explained well by Ted Byfield. He believed – as did many others – that such change would enable the Senate to properly represent provincial interests. In particular, this could be achieved by the creation of a "Triple-E" Senate:

By instituting a Senate in which all provinces were Equally represented, which was Elected, and which was Effective in that it could veto the Commons. With such a Triple-E Senate in place, the NEP would never have been proposed, let alone passed. This was the protection which the Canadian constitution denied. This must be the West's objective (Byfield 1991, 4).

Of course, Senate reform involves changing Canada's constitution. Unfortunately, constitutional changes can only be made with the support of central Canada, and that region has absolutely no interest in changes that will give the West more power.

Nevertheless, during the 1980s and 1990s considerable efforts were made by Westerners who wanted Senate reform.

The campaign to adopt a Triple-E Senate is described by Preston Manning in his book, *The New Canada*.

As he explains, during the conflict between Alberta and Pierre Trudeau over oil pricing in the mid-1970s, Premier Peter Lougheed created a Citizens' Advisory Committee on the Constitution to make recommendations to the provincial government.

Gene Dais, a University of Calgary professor of constitutional law, was on the committee. Dais convinced other committee members that the representation of regional interests in the national government could be improved if the Senate became an elected body with an equal number of senators from each province. As a result, "Senate reform" became a priority for the Alberta government.

In 1981 the Canada West Foundation published a significant proposal for a Triple-E Senate entitled, *Regional*

Representation: The Canadian Partnership. It was written by Dr. Peter McCormick of the University of Lethbridge, Gordon Gibson, a former executive assistant to Prime Minister Pierre Trudeau, and Senator Ernest Manning, a former premier of Alberta.

Subsequently, an Alberta Committee for an Elected Senate was created to promote the idea in 1983. As Preston Manning writes,

> Bert Brown, a farmer and political activist from the town of Kathryn, was elected as chairman. Ted Byfield coined the shorthand phrase "Triple-E" to summarize the committee's Senate reform proposals. When interest in the committee's work spread to Saskatchewan and British Columbia, its name was changed to the Canadian Committee for a Triple-E Senate (Manning 1992, 197).

The Alberta Progressive Conservative Party endorsed the Triple-E Senate proposal at a 1984 convention, and in March 1985 the Alberta government's Special Select Committee on Senate Reform called for the government to officially embrace the Triple-E Senate concept.

After Don Getty became premier in 1985, he committed his government to support the Triple-E Senate. Indeed, in 1988 he appointed a Senate Reform Task Force to promote the Triple-E Senate concept to the other provinces.

Getty's support for Senate reform led to Alberta holding Canada's first Senate candidate election in October 1989, which was won by Stan Waters of the Reform Party. Prime Minister Brian Mulroney reluctantly appointed Waters to the Senate.

Then, in 1993, the Reform Party – with a slogan of "the West wants in" and a commitment to the Triple-E Senate – won 52 seats in the federal election. From a Western perspective, it looked like the Triple-E Senate idea was on a roll.

But it was not to be.

Why not?

Because the federal government does not care what reforms Alberta wants for the political system.

Alberta is a bit player on constitutional matters and its proposals can safely be ignored by Ottawa. This is what history demonstrates.

Writing over thirty years ago, University of Calgary political scientist Roger Gibbins accurately describes the situation:

> From the early institutional radicalism of the United Farmers of Alberta and the economic radicalism of Social Credit through the Senate reformers of the last decade and the Reform Party of Canada, Albertans have again and again challenged the constitutional and institutional organization of Canadian political life. What is striking, however, is that the Alberta challenge has had little if any impact on the national scene. The national preoccupation with Quebec has been so pervasive and so complete that Alberta initiatives for *institutional reform* have gone all but unnoticed (Gibbins 1992, 81).

Consider the historical lesson carefully: Alberta's initiatives to reform Canada's political system go "unnoticed." Alberta has no political leverage to create the change it wants.

That was true with the Alberta PCs in the 1980s, the Reform Party in the 1990s, and it's still true today. The lesson of history is that Alberta's campaigns for institutional reform have always failed.

Conclusion

For decades Albertans have been unhappy with the province's situation within Canada. Many of them have been involved in campaigns to improve that situation, through initiatives like the Reform Party of Canada and the Canadian Committee for a Triple-E Senate. These were noble efforts but they did not succeed due to resistance from central Canada. Alberta – and the West in general – does not have the electoral weight necessary to achieve meaningful reforms.

Even today, though, many Albertans still believe that Canada's political system can be reformed so the province's voice could be heard in the national government. Indeed, some people are working towards this goal even now. Let's get more representation for the West in Ottawa, they say.

This is a noble goal, for sure, but one that will never be achieved. This chapter – and the next – show that there is a long history of Albertans trying unsuccessfully to reform the system. Unfortunately, current efforts along those lines will be just as fruitless as before.

This is also a lesson Stephen Harper learned when he was prime minister. For example, he was committed to Senate reform, but his efforts to achieve it were thwarted every step of the way. Ultimately, the Supreme Court of Canada put an end to Harper's attempts at Senate reform.

When it came to Senate reform, as well as other matters favoured by the West, Harper ended up being unable to break out of the "Laurentian Consensus."

Chapter 5 - Constitutional Reform is Not Going to Happen

Despite the best efforts of the Reform Party and others, Senate reform did not even come close in the 1990s. However, after the Reform Party was transformed into the Canadian Alliance, one of the original Reformers, Stephen Harper, became the Canadian Alliance leader. He helped merge the Canadian Alliance with the Progressive Conservative Party of Canada in 2003 to form the new Conservative Party of Canada. He also became leader of that new party.

Then, in 2006, he was elected prime minister.

After winning the 2006 election, Harper aggressively pursued Senate reform using the powers at his disposal. As University of Ottawa professor Adam Dodek puts it, "From the moment it took office in February 2006, the Harper Government indicated its intention to act on its promise of Senate reform" (Dodek 2015, 640).

It first acted on that promise by introducing a Senate reform bill in the Senate in May 2006. Harper personally appeared before the Senate committee studying the bill, demonstrating his intense commitment to this issue.

In December 2006 his government introduced a Senate reform bill into the House of Commons. Had it passed, this bill would have authorized "consultative elections" whereby voters could select nominees whose names would be submitted to the prime minister to consider when filling Senate seats.

These bills died but Senate reform legislation was frequently reintroduced while Harper was in power. During his first seven years in office, three such bills were introduced into the Senate and five into the House of Commons. This clearly indicated a genuine commitment to pursuing Senate reform.

> Besides such legislative efforts, Dodek notes that in July 2007, the Prime Minister appointed Bert Brown to the Senate; Brown had attracted national attention in the early 1980s by plowing "Triple E Senate or Else" into his neighbour's field. Brown was also the only person to run in each of Alberta's three Senate nominees' elections in 1989, 1998 and 2004, winning a spot as a "Senator-in-waiting" in both 1998 and 2004 (Dodek 2015, 644).

In May 2012, the Québec government initiated a reference case on one of the Senate reform bills, asking its own Court of Appeal to rule on the constitutionality of "consultative elections" and Harper's plan to impose nine-year term limits on Senators.

In response, Harper's government initiated its own reference case to the Supreme Court of Canada so that it could frame the questions the court would consider. As Dodek explains, "the decision to bring the reference can be seen as both a reaction to the Government of Québec and as a proactive strike to get ahead of the Québec Court of Appeal decision" (Dodek 2015, 656).

To make a long story short, the Supreme Court decided that Senate reform of the kind desired by Harper would require a constitutional amendment. This brought his government's Senate reform agenda to a screeching halt. The Senate reference decision essentially put an end to Senate reform in Canada.

Dodek writes that one way to understand this whole episode is to see a man dedicated to Senate reform finding "that once he became Prime Minister his attempts at Senate reform were thwarted at every step of the way: first by the opposition and the Senate itself, next by some within his own caucus, by the provincial premiers, and finally by the courts, notably the Supreme Court of Canada" (Dodek 2015, 671).

So there you have it. Stephen Harper – a man who was committed to constitutional reform to benefit the West – became prime minister and over a period of years used every tool at his disposal to reform the Senate. But he could not prevail in the face of intense opposition from central Canada.

If Stephen Harper couldn't do it then it can't be done.

Albertans must realize that their best and brightest went to Ottawa to fix the system but the system couldn't be fixed. Spending the next few years trying to reform Canada's constitution would end in failure and frustration, as it always has in the past. No one will be able to top Harper's efforts.

Stephen Harper couldn't overcome the Laurentian Consensus

Stephen Harper was the best prime minister of the last several decades. Nevertheless, what he was able to accomplish was quite limited from a conservative and western Canadian perspective. That's because the only way to achieve and maintain power is to cater to the people of central Canada. Central Canadians are not particularly sympathetic to conservative ideals, and especially not sympathetic to the aspirations of western Canada.

The fact of the matter is that the interests of central Canada determine the important policy initiatives of the federal government, regardless of whether the Liberals or Conservatives are in power.

This is the conclusion of University of Toronto political scientist Andrew McDougall. In 2020 he wrote an article to determine what the "Laurentian Consensus" involves, and whether the Trudeau Liberals can be described as governing in accordance with that Consensus. He concludes, of course, that Trudeau does represent the Laurentian Consensus. But perhaps surprisingly, he also concludes that Stephen Harper followed the Laurentian Consensus while he was prime minister.

McDougall defines the Laurentian Consensus as being an "area of historically overlapping political agreement between the federal Liberals and Conservatives over how best to govern the country and its institutions, which for electoral reasons has required them to place the interests of Ontario and Quebec at the centre of their agenda" (McDougall 2020, 12).

In terms of policies, this means "an economic agenda that benefits Ontario and Quebec at the expense of the rest of the country" along with basic welfare state measures such as government-provided pensions as well as government health care and a commitment to bilingualism.

Besides the actual policy agenda, the consensus involves having "real political power over national problems being decided disproportionately by elites in Toronto, Ottawa, Montreal, and Quebec City" (McDougall 2020, 13).

In sum, the Laurentian Consensus is "rooted in protecting the interests of politically dominant Central Canada, its elites, and its view of how to govern the country" (McDougall 2020, 20).

In recent years, the policy agenda of the Laurentian Consensus has involved measures to fight climate change, such as the carbon tax and official support for the Paris Agreement. These policies disproportionately harm the oil-producing provinces – namely Alberta and Saskatchewan – thus the people of Ontario and Quebec can support them wholeheartedly without personally suffering negative economic consequences.

The fact that the Trudeau government reflects the Laurentian Consensus is unmistakable and unsurprising.

But the role of Stephen Harper in upholding the Laurentian Consensus is rather surprising. McDougall concludes that while Harper was openly supportive of Alberta and the West, "there is not much to suggest that in substance his government was genuinely Western to the *detriment* of Central Canada, however much he disagreed with many of the tenets of the Laurentian Consensus" (McDougall 2020, 30).

This was because of the political reality of Canada. To win power, a party must appeal to the voters of Ontario and

Quebec. This was just as true for Stephen Harper as anyone else. When he won a majority government in 2011, he had 73 MPs from Ontario, and a combined 72 from the four western provinces. MPs from Ontario, therefore, dominated his caucus.

To some degree Harper furthered policies favouring the West, but as McDougall notes,
> on most of the bigger issues on which the Laurentian Consensus rests and which he criticized as a Reform Party member, namely the value of social programs, the composition of national institutions, or asymmetrical federalism when it comes to Quebec in Canada, his reforms were either moderate, of limited scope, or were issues he refused to touch at all (McDougall 2020, 32).

McDougall explains that "Stephen Harper knew the limits of trying to escape the Laurentian Consensus. At its base, it embodies the values that are in the interests of the political elites of the largest provinces of Ontario and Quebec" (McDougall 2020, 33).

The implications of this are clear. Even if the West helps to elect a favourable Conservative government, that government will support the interests of the Laurentian Consensus. There is no way out of this because a party must win a large number of seats in Ontario and Quebec in order to form government. Pierre Poilievre cannot avoid this either.

Stephen Harper was a pro-West prime minister, but the system does not allow a government to escape the calculation needed to win power, namely, catering to the interests of central Canada.

When even a prime minister as sympathetic to the West as Stephen Harper can't break away from the Laurentian Consensus, it's clear that achieving independence is the only reasonable option left for Alberta to pursue freedom and prosperity.

Andrew McDougall isn't the only one to have noticed Stephen Harper's compromise on core issues. Years earlier, political scientist Tom Flanagan of the University of Calgary explained Harper's transformation after becoming prime minister. Although being elected as a pro-West conservative, Harper's government did not differ in many respects from the Liberals:

> Harper has adopted the Liberal shibboleths of bilingualism and multiculturalism. He has no plans to reintroduce capital punishment, criminalize abortion, repeal gay marriage or repeal the Charter. He swears allegiance to the *Canada Health Act*. He has enriched equalization payments for the provinces and pogey for individuals. He has enthusiastically accepted government subsidies to business, while enlarging regional economic expansion. He now advocates Keynesian deficit spending and government bailouts of failing corporations, at least part of the time (Flanagan 2011, 30).

Note especially Flanagan's point that Harper "has enriched equalization payments for the provinces." This refers to the fact that Harper increased the transfers of money from Alberta to other provinces, especially Quebec. To put this most crassly, because he wanted to win a majority government and remain in power, he had to buy the favour of central Canada with Alberta's money.

Alberta is Canada's cash cow

University of Calgary political scientist Barry Cooper cites the maxim, "Canadian elections have become opportunities for Ontario to decide how much money the West will send to Quebec" (Cooper 2020, 218). It's funny, but it contains a lot of truth.

Regardless of whether Conservatives or Liberals form the government, Alberta contributes billions of extra dollars annually to the federal coffers, and Quebec receives billions of extra dollars from those coffers.

The federal government has a number of programs that, in effect, redistribute money from wealthier provinces – especially Alberta – to poorer provinces. Among these programs are the Canada Health Transfer (CHT) and Canada Social Transfer (CST). But the most prominent and controversial is the equalization program which provides money to poorer provinces so they can provide their citizens with public services comparable to the wealthier provinces.

The history and details of equalization are explained in the book, *Fiscal Federalism and Equalization Policy in Canada: Political and Economic Dimensions* written by Professor Daniel Béland along with four of his academic colleagues.

As they explain, the equalization program was originally created in 1957. Then in 1982, without any controversy, the principle of equalization was constitutionalized.

Indeed, the principle of equalization is widely accepted among federal politicians. Béland et al write that although the Reform Party wanted the program to be more targeted, "all the federal parties supported equalization, possibly in part because of the electoral weight of receiving provinces" (Béland et al 2017, 26).

That latter phrase is key. All the major federal parties want to win seats in Québec, which carries a lot of "electoral weight." Any party advocating less equalization to Québec will be shut out of power.

Even Stephen Harper's Conservative government catered to Québec on this matter.

In March 2005, the Liberal government of Paul Martin created a panel to review the equalization program. It delivered its report in May 2006, after Harper had become prime minister. The report's recommendations displeased the resource-rich provinces, but Harper implemented those recommendations anyway.

As Béland et al explain, "From a political standpoint, implementing the recommendations meant more money for Québec, a province the Conservatives were courting at the time in an effort to secure a majority government at the next federal election" (Béland et al 2017, 38).

Another factor favouring Québec is that the monetary benefits of that province's hydroelectricity are not factored into equalization. In essence, Québec's formal fiscal capacity, which is used to calculate how much it will receive, is artificially lowered "by allowing provincially owned Hydro-Québec to charge consumers, especially large industrial ones, a price far below the market value" (Béland et al 2017, 43).

In this way, the equalization program "provides incentives for the Québec government to keep its prices and royalties low" (Béland et al 2017, 43).

Another way to put this is that Québec cheats the system in order to get more money from Alberta.

Québec, of course, receives more money from the equalization program than any other province. On a per capita basis, some of the smaller provinces receive larger amounts, but in terms of total dollars, Québec gets the most.

Béland et al summarize the Québec proportion of total equalization payments this way: "Over the 1980-81 to 2015-16 time period, the smallest percentage going to [Québec] was 38 per cent in 2004-05, and the largest was 60 per cent in 2008-09. However, most years fall into a narrow band of 45-55 per cent" (Béland et al 2017, 66).

The fact that Québec benefits disproportionately creates resentment among some people in the West. Béland et al write that this situation is "allegedly related to the threat of separation and the need for federal parties to win seats in the province. From this perspective, equalization is frequently understood as a program that funnels enormous amounts of money to Quebec for purely partisan electoral reasons" (Béland et al 2017, 47).

Although they use the word "allegedly" in that statement, they subsequently acknowledge the reality of the situation when they explain that
> equalization has most likely helped federalists in Québec make the case against the independence of the province. In fact, the economic argument in favour of Québec remaining part of Canada has often featured references, sometimes explicit and other times implicit, to the equalization program as important to the financing of the province's social programs (Béland et al 2017, 111).

To put this same point much more crassly, equalization payments are used to bribe Québec to remain in Canada. If it were to leave Canada, Québec would lose billions of dollars a year in free money – most of which has been taken from Alberta.

Let's face it. As long as Alberta remains in Canada this will be the case. None of the major federal parties will challenge the equalization program because that would mean losing support in Québec. This goes for Pierre Poilievre and the Conservative Party as well.

Conclusion

Alberta is Canada's cash cow and its whipping boy. Changing the boss in Ottawa won't make much difference because it's the political system that guarantees central Canada's dominance. This is clearly seen in the case of Stephen Harper, who sincerely wanted to help the West but had his hands tied by the system.

Again, independence would solve the problem by putting Albertans in control of their own destiny and prevent the constant transfer of their money to the provinces that have "electoral weight."

The decades of mistreatment that Alberta has experienced within Canada has led to a phenomenon widely known as "western alienation." Although that term is far from ideal, it refers to a distinctive aspect of political culture that contributes to the sense of Alberta being different from much of the rest of the country.

Chapter 6 - The West is Different from the Rest of Canada

Most of this book focuses on economic issues, especially the transfer of money or resources to central Canada at Alberta's expense. Alberta is often on the losing end of federal government policies because it does not carry enough "electoral weight" to make a difference. Therefore, independence is Alberta's best path forward.

Partly because of its geographic distance from central Canada, partly because of its different historical experiences than central Canada, and partly because of its historic mistreatment within Canada, there has long been a sense in Alberta that the West is somehow different from the rest of Canada. It's not always easy to articulate the difference, and there are few data sets – other than federal election results – that clearly demonstrate any notable differences. Yet, the perception of Western distinctiveness persists.

Occasionally, attempts are made to communicate this sense of difference. In 2002, University of Calgary sociologist

Harry Hiller provided some indication of it through a personal encounter:

> A recent migrant to Calgary from an Eastern province remarked to me recently, 'You really get a very different view of Canada from living in the West and in Calgary.' This person went on to remark that whether it was the mountains, Calgary's unique Co-op, the Reform party, the Flames, or the predominant energy sector, there was a different feel to living in Calgary in terms of how people viewed the world and how social life was organized (Hiller 2002, 35).

Gerald Friesen, a history professor at the University of Manitoba, has also written about Western distinctiveness. He recounts his experience of being in central Canada during a period from 1996-97. While there, he found that many Easterners questioned Westerners' commitment to Canada. As he explains, "It was as if the views being expressed by the West's makers of public policy and elected representatives no longer struck a chord with other Canadians. Or as if the issues and choices being debated in the West did not reflect Canadian values" (Friesen 1999).

This perception was reinforced when the director of the McGill Institute for the Study of Canada, Desmond Morton, suggested to Friesen that the country was drifting apart and that the West was not understood in the East.

That view was emphasized again by some commentators at a 1998 conference on "Accommodating the New West." At that conference,

> Gordon Gibson, journalist and former politician,
> Tom Flanagan, political scientist at the University of Calgary, and Doug Owram, historian at the University

of Alberta, asserted that the East seemed unwilling to accommodate the West, that the gulf between the two was larger than most people appreciated and that conversation across the divide had become difficult, if not impossible (Friesen 1999).

That event occurred over twenty years ago, when the Reform Party of Canada – the party of the West – was the official opposition in Parliament. Today, the gulf between the West (Alberta and Saskatchewan, anyway) and the Eastern provinces is likely even greater.

Writing in 1999, Friesen described the general outlook of Albertans as follows:

> Albertans see themselves as entrepreneurial, and their culture is, indeed, more supportive of economic enterprise and individual productivity than any other in Canada. It seems that every conversation notes at least one "amazing inspirational testimonial" wherein a former gas-field worker or building caretaker begins knitting toques or molding chocolate mints in a disused shed and – boom! – is now worth a million, maybe two. The image sits at the heart of this distinctive culture. The Albertan does not emphasize the delightful and different quality of the province's natural environment, as does the British Columbian, but rather the vigour and competitiveness and the go-it-alone quality of its residents (Friesen 1999, 86-87).

Friesen also considers how recent historical events have impacted Alberta's political culture. Unlike most historical events – which citizens tend to forget quickly – the National Energy Program (NEP) and its effects still loom large in the minds of many Albertans. As Friesen puts it,

> The bust, or recession, of 1981-87 seared its image into the hearts of Albertans. The only explanation of the crisis that has survived in the public memory is that Ottawa – Pierre Trudeau and his French Canadian allies, notably Energy Minister Marc Lalonde – caused the collapse. It would be fair to say that the turmoil of the 1980s stands out more sharply in the public memory of Albertans than does the Great Depression of the 1930s (Friesen 1999, 89).

Besides Pierre Trudeau's attack on Alberta in the 1980s, another event that left its mark on Alberta's political culture was the effort by Premier Ralph Klein to aggressively reduce government spending. As Friesen writes, Klein's so-called revolution "consolidated the self-perception of Albertans as the frontiersmen and -women who dared to live differently and, by taking such risks, who dared to prosper" (Friesen 1999, 90).

Indeed, Klein's policies "appealed to two populist emotions in Alberta—the frontier preference for small government and the entrepreneurial delight in low taxes" (Friesen 1999, 92).

It is true, though, as Friesen points out, that Alberta is not a homogeneous conservative community. Besides the strong base of conservatives, there are also many active – and increasingly influential – left-wing activists and sympathizers in the province.

Nevertheless, historically, Alberta's political culture has manifested distinctive features that distinguish it from the other provinces. It is those features that form the basis for Friesen's description of Alberta's uniqueness. Thus, there is a basis for believing – as many people sense – that Alberta is somewhat different culturally from the rest of Canada.

The creation of regional identity

People who live in a particular geographical territory generally share certain common political interests. For example, due to the significant role that oil and gas fills in Alberta's economy, all Albertans have a common interest in the success of the petroleum industry. Even those who are not directly involved in that industry benefit from the prosperity it brings to the province.

Government programs funded by resource revenues are one of the most obvious ways all Albertans benefit from oil and gas.

However, just because the people of a particular region share certain common political interests doesn't necessarily mean that everyone understands the common interests and works to defend them. Someone needs to intellectually formulate an understanding of those interests and express them publicly.

This is explained by University of Calgary sociologist Harry Hiller. Hiller points out that regional perspectives can only develop when regional interests become politicized.

Hiller explains as follows:
> Since regionalism involves a world view based on territoriality, it is partially natural and partially the result of framing; that is, some person or group must sharply articulate and thus 'frame' the perspective. In that sense, regionalism becomes political and requires the mobilization of support. This means that while the regionalist perspective will be commonly known and available to residents of a territory, it may exist in a submerged state until it is triggered by changing conditions and circumstances (Hiller 2002, 34).

In other words, although there are natural common interests among the people of a certain territory, people are not mobilized in defence of those interests until those interests have been articulated. The articulation of those interests provides an interpretive framework to help people understand the issues at stake and how they are affected.

For example, the view that Alberta and the other prairie provinces have been mistreated within Canada was already being articulated early in the province's history. This view has provided a kind of cultural bond among Albertans and other Westerners over many decades because it conveys a shared experience. Although the term is severely deficient, this shared feeling of mistreatment is commonly referred to as "western alienation."

Western alienation as a component of regional identity

Whenever people in the West become upset about a federal policy or another election win by the Liberal Party of Canada, that response is frequently described as a re-occurrence of the phenomenon of "western alienation." So, what is that?

University of Calgary political scientist Roger Gibbins describes the concept of "western alienation" as "a political ideology of regional discontent" (Gibbins 1980, 169).

To a large degree, it represents generations of frustration with the way western Canada has been excluded from economic and political power:

> Western alienation encompasses a sense of political, economic and, to a lesser extent, cultural estrangement from the Canadian heartland. The ideological content of western alienation, of course, has not remained constant over time; the attitudinal baggage of beliefs,

grievances and perceptions has changed as the conditions of the prairie society have changed. Yet at the same time there is great continuity with the past, continuity expressed through the interlocking themes that western Canada is always outgunned in national politics and that as a consequence has been subjected to varying degrees of economic exploitation by central Canada (Gibbins 1980, 169).

This sentiment became especially pronounced after Pierre Trudeau became prime minister in the late 1960s. A key aspect of Trudeau's political program was to defeat Quebec nationalism by making Quebeckers feel at home right across the country. Part of this program involved the Official Languages Act in 1969, to make French more prevalent from coast to coast.

Before the energy wars erupted toward the end of 1973, Trudeau's emphasis on catering to Quebec was the main reason many Westerners didn't like him. As Gibbins notes, "The focal point of western Canadian hostility in the 70s was the bilingualism and biculturalism program of the federal government" (Gibbins 1980, 178). He goes on to write that, "On the Prairies opposition to bilingualism and biculturalism, and to the strengthened French Canadian presence in Ottawa, fits neatly into and reinforces pre-existing antipathies towards the central government itself" (Gibbins 1980, 180).

Overall, the content of long-term Western frustration and anger towards central Canada can be summarized as follows:
Western alienation constitutes a regionally-distinct political culture through and within which are expressed economic discontent, the rejection of a semi-colonial status within the Canadian state, antipathy

towards Quebec and French Canadian influence within the national government, the irritation of the West's partisan weakness within a succession of Liberal national governments, and the demand from provincial political elites for greater jurisdiction autonomy (Gibbins 1980, 191).

Western alienation: An Eastern Marxist concept

The generations-long frustration and anger that many Westerners have felt towards central Canada is a sincere and deep-seated sentiment. Nevertheless, some patriotic Westerners have objected to using the term "western alienation" to describe that sentiment.

For decades, Professor Barry Cooper of the University of Calgary has been a prominent intellectual defender of Alberta and the West. More than anyone else, he has written about the distinct political identity of the prairie West. Importantly, Cooper has challenged the notion of "western alienation" because it misconstrues western political culture.

Cooper traces the concept of alienation to the 1953 book *Democracy in Alberta* written by C. B. Macpherson. Macpherson was a very influential Marxist political scientist at the University of Toronto. He analyzed Alberta's Social Credit movement and did not like what he saw. As Cooper notes, "Macpherson's book set the stage for a half-century of unflattering interpretation of Alberta and the West" (Cooper 2009, 114-115).

Macpherson claimed that democracy in Alberta was degenerate and that a dictatorial government could develop. In his view, Alberta was a bad place because its people did not adopt the supposed insights of Marxism. Cooper notes,

"As early as 1953, then, the argument that combined envy at the resource revenue of the province with distaste for the way Albertans conduct their political affairs was fast congealing into a cliché" (Cooper 2009, 115).

Macpherson died in 1987 but his work lives on. As Cooper points out, "In his deeply flawed book can be found the source of the other great cliché of western politics: alienation" (Cooper 2009, 117-118).

In short, Cooper claims that the concept of "western alienation" was fabricated by left-wing eastern intellectuals. It was not developed in the West: "The fact is, western alienation does not describe westerners' sense of regional identity so far as they are concerned" (Cooper 2009, 121).

Nevertheless, it is a widely used concept and Cooper explains why:

> It permits non-westerners to overlook the substance of western interests and pride in the regional interpretation of them; it allows non-westerners to recast the conflict of those interests and the interpretation of them into the more congenial form of a marginalized discourse. Westerners, they can say with a clear conscience, look at matters differently than we genuine, which is to say, Laurentian, Canadians. All the fuss "out there" stems from "alienation," which is both a definitive put-down because the term used to be understood as synonymous with madness (these alienated westerners better consult an alienist) and sufficiently abstract to preclude the necessity of any further investigation (Cooper 2009, 121-122).

Historically, many informed Westerners have been angered by the harmful policies of the federal government and other eastern institutions. But this does not amount to alienation. It is the justifiable indignation at injustice. Classifying it as alienation is essentially a way of dismissing the legitimate grievances of the West.

Cooper writes,
> Westerners have not been "alienated" from the central institutions of power in Canada so much as excluded. Initially they were excluded by subordinate legal status, then by economic subordination, and more recently by the majoritarian character of the federal government that has never reconciled conflicting regional interests so much as identified the national interest with Laurentian Canada (Cooper 2009, 122).

Professor George Melnyk

Another University of Calgary professor, George Melnyk, also sees "western alienation" as a concept developed by easterners. Interestingly, despite being sympathetic to the West, Melnyk is left-wing and he's horrified by the right-wing pro-Western movements of the past.

Nevertheless, like Cooper, he helpfully explains how the terminology of alienation subordinates the West's legitimate concerns to central Canada:
> Alienation came to be a general term covering everything negative about the region from Western separatists to Lougheed's blue-eyed sheiks and anti-Francophone bigotry. Alienation came to represent a threat to the centre and to nationhood. It was not important what Westerners felt about themselves; it was important that they were alienated from the centre where all goodness lay. It was Westerners who were alienated, while Central Canadians were not. The

burden of deviancy was the West's (Melnyk 1993, 119).

He explains this point further by noting that the "alienation image rejects the nostalgic identity generated by Westerners about themselves, and replaces it with only one concern—alienation from the only true self, Canada. No other self counts. In the alienation image, Canada is the central focus, and the West a disenchanted hinterland" (Melnyk 1993, 119-120).

As a result, much like Cooper, Melnyk rejects "the alienation theme because it is fundamentally anti-Western and externally imposed" (Melnyk 1993, 121).

In times like today when the federal government is engaging in policies that are especially harmful to the West, the media commonly tout "western alienation" as the explanation for westerners' resentment. That term is so common and ingrained that it's hard to avoid using.

Nevertheless, understanding that it's an externally imposed concept that subordinates the West's concerns, and even dismisses the West's concerns, should help Westerners to reconsider its usefulness.

Conclusion

In some respects, Alberta's political culture differs from most other parts of Canada. Although some of this is the result of geography and different historical experiences, the mistreatment of the West contributes to an aspect of political culture most frequently described as "western alienation."

That term is ubiquitous in discussions about Western dissatisfaction with the federal government. Nevertheless, some Western intellectuals reject the term because it describes central Canadians' perceptions of the West's concerns rather than the way Westerners perceive their own situation.

"Western alienation" terminology is not going away and will continue to be used widely in the media. But Westerners should be aware of its deficiencies in describing their frustration and anger toward the federal government. Even with its deficiencies, though, it does point toward a genuine sentiment experience by many Westerners. And it is that sentiment that fuels the desire for Alberta independence.

Chapter 7 – Fear for the Future

Some people argue that any move towards a more autonomous or independent Alberta will be economically ruinous. They say defending the province from Canadian centralism will create political instability that scares away businesses and talented people.

The example cited as evidence for their point is Quebec after the election of the Parti Québécois (PQ) in 1976. The PQ is a separatist party with a stated goal of making Quebec independent. In the years immediately following its election, tens of thousands of people left Quebec along with many businesses, resulting in severe economic decline.

Supporters of the status quo say that an assertive Alberta will suffer a similar fate. However, when they use the Quebec example, they don't tell the whole story. Viewed more carefully, it's clear that the Quebec case does not support their argument.

This is apparent in an article by Prof. Duane Bratt of Mount Royal University where he argues that Alberta is about to suffer economically due to the *Alberta Sovereignty Within a United Canada Act*. As he puts it, "Unfortunately for Quebec, threatening separatism and adopting autonomy policies meant that the province suffered population decline and capital flight" (Bratt 2022).

He correctly explains that, "In 1970, Montreal was Canada's most populous city and Quebec had 28 per cent of Canada's population. By 1980, Toronto had surpassed Montreal in size and Quebec's share of Canada's population had dropped to 26.5 per cent" (Bratt 2022).

The key "autonomy measure" identified by Prof. Bratt was Bill 101, the so-called Charter of the French Language. This piece of legislation is the key to understanding Quebec's business and population loss. Passed in 1977, Bill 101 imposed severe restrictions on the use of languages other than French in various spheres of Quebec life, including education and business. Suppressing English, of course, was the main goal.

The PQ government's message to English-speaking people in Quebec was loud and clear: we don't want your stinking language in our province. Therefore, English-speakers left in large numbers, along with their money and their businesses.

As an article in The Metric explains,
After the passage of Bill 101, Quebec suffered a drastic economic downturn. The labor force shrank, as anglophones and allophones (those who speak neither English nor French) departed for other provinces. Jobs also left Quebec, as several companies moved their major operations from Quebec to neighboring Ontario, especially to Toronto. This movement helped Toronto surpass Montreal as the economic hub of Canada (Jiang 2018).

The online *Canadian Encyclopedia* emphasizes how Quebec's language law helped boost Toronto. Bill 101, it says, "prodded as many as 150,000 well off, educated, fully-employed English-speaking Montrealers to choose the 401 over 101 – and to remove themselves, their jobs, their savings and their children from the province rather than face the prospect of having to learn to speak French" (Aubin 2007).

In other words, the key factor in Quebec's decline was government-imposed language restrictions. Many people did not want to be forced to live their lives in French. Instead, they wanted to be free to use English or some other language.

Therefore, to compare Bill 101 to the *Alberta Sovereignty Within a United Canada Act* is utterly baseless. No one in Alberta will be forced to use a particular language or to live a certain way to uphold Alberta's culture. This means that the main driver of Quebec's economic decline has no parallels in Alberta, and an exodus from Alberta is not on the horizon.

Alberta is much friendlier to business than Quebec was in the late 1970s. Furthermore, Alberta has one of the world's largest oil deposits, and the world needs oil. Oil companies won't be moving out any time soon.

Using scare tactics and fear is common in politics. To compare the *Alberta Sovereignty Within a United Canada Act* or proposals for an independent Alberta to Quebec's Bill 101 is an attempt to generate fear and anxiety. The goal is to convince Albertans to support the status quo and not resist federal plans to harm the province's economy.

Climate change and Alberta's oil

There are also those who experience fear and anxiety due to climate change, which is said to be caused by the burning of fossil fuels. These people say that Alberta must do its part to prevent climate change, and this involves going along with the phase-out of oil and natural gas. The carbon released from burning fossil fuels is heating up the earth and will result in disaster, they claim. Thankfully, we have alternative energy sources such as wind and solar power. Problem solved.

It all sounds so good until reality sets in.

The truth is, wind and solar power cannot replace the energy needed for a modern industrial society. Sure, green energy sources can produce some energy, and that's better than nothing. But with current technology, they are nowhere near being able to replace the vast, reliable, and dependable energy we get from fossil fuels.

At least this is the view of the well-respected geopolitical strategist, Peter Zeihan. Many Albertans first heard of Zeihan a few years ago when he wrote a book, *The Accidental Superpower*, arguing that Alberta would be better off joining the United States.

His most recent book is *The End of the World Is Just the Beginning: Mapping the Collapse of Globalization*. In it he describes what he believes will occur in the world economy over the next decade or two. It's not pretty, because he expects the post-World War Two international trading system – which he calls the "Order" – to be disrupted, leading to hardships for many countries.

The good news is that Canada and the United States are best suited to weather the storm because North America uniquely has the resources to be self-sufficient in energy, food production and manufacturing.

One topic he discusses is climate change and fossil fuels. Zeihan himself is convinced that climate change is happening and that it's being driven by human activity like the burning of fossil fuels. In fact, his own home in Colorado is powered by solar panels. He's a true believer in green energy technology, which he simply calls "greentech."

That is, Zeihan holds "progressive" views on global warming and the need to transition away from fossil fuels. But as a geopolitical strategist, he must deal with reality, not with wishful thinking. To maintain the respect his business depends on, he has to tell the cold, hard truth, and not entertain fantasies of environmental utopia.

Zeihan understands that the current lifestyles and standards of living of most people in the world require oil, and this will not soon change. As he puts it, "**we are nowhere near being 'done' with oil**" (Zeihan 2022, 263 – emphasis in the original).

Zeihan is all in favour of wind and solar power. But as he points out, most parts of the world do not have enough wind or sunshine to make those alternatives viable: "The unfortunate fact is that greentech in its current form simply isn't useful for most people in most places—either to reduce carbon emissions *or* to provide a substitute for energy inputs in a more chaotic, post-Order world" (Zeihan 2022, 265).

Even in those places where greentech is viable, it is not reliable. The sun doesn't always shine, and the wind doesn't always blow. This means that "greentech today is so unreliable in most locations that those localities that do attempt greentech have no choice but to maintain a full conventional system for their total peak demand—at full cost" (Zeihan 2022, 271).

Greentech does produce a growing amount of energy, but in its current form it can – at best – reduce fossil fuel demand by about a dozen percentage points.

Fossil fuels are quite remarkable, when you think about it. Zeihan writes, "Fossil fuels are so concentrated that they are literally 'energy' in physical form" (Zeihan 2022, 268). By contrast, greentech requires lots of space for solar panels and wind turbines.

The long and short of it is that fossil fuels will continue to be the dominant forms of energy for the foreseeable future. Sure, there are a few places where wind and solar can make a difference, but as Zeihan notes, "Nearly all other locations will remain dependent upon more traditional fuels for the vast majority of their energy needs" (Zeihan 2022, 275).

Therefore, the reports of the imminent death of fossil fuels are greatly exaggerated. This is good news for Alberta. Our oil and gas will remain in high demand for a long time to come. There is no reason to expect a transition to other sources of energy in the near future because we don't yet have an alternative energy source that can do the job.

Climate change and authoritarian politics

Besides the desire to phase out fossil fuels, another concerning aspect of the climate change agenda is the potential to use the "climate crisis" to justify the elimination of historic rights and liberties.

In 2021, Ross Mittiga, an assistant professor of political science at the Catholic University of Chile, wrote an article for the *American Political Science Review*, one of the most respected academic journals in the world. This article provides a rationale for progressive politicians to run roughshod over almost all of the historic rights and liberties enjoyed by people living in democratic countries.

Mittiga is not Chilean, he just happens to teach in Chile. He is an American and a Democratic Party activist. In fact, his 2017 campaign to get the Democratic Party nomination for a seat in the Virginia House of Delegates garnered the attention of the *Washington Post*. His views undoubtedly represent a segment of North American progressivism.

Mittiga argues that the foundational premise of political legitimacy requires a government to protect its citizens. A government that cannot ensure the safety of its citizens loses its legitimacy. Therefore, since – in his view – climate change is such a dangerous threat, government may rightfully resort to authoritarian methods to prevent it. Authoritarian powers will enable governments to guarantee safety and thereby maintain their legitimacy.

As Mittiga puts it, "having a government unencumbered by democratic procedures or constitutional limits on power could be advantageous when it comes to implementing urgently needed climate action" (Mittiga 2021).

According to Mittiga, freedom is a threat to progressive climate policies. Why? Well, for one thing, in some countries referenda or public protests have been used to defeat carbon taxes. Besides that, free speech protections have enabled people who are skeptical of climate change to communicate their concerns to others. Furthermore, individual autonomy has allowed people to maintain their regular diets rather than changing to climate-friendly foods. In other words, with freedom, people live and talk in ways that do not conform to progressive ideals.

Since for progressives freedom is the problem, it must be restricted – permanently. Mittiga writes that "the climate crisis may not just lead to temporary and localized suspensions of (for example) democratic processes or individual rights but precipitate a more substantial and enduring shift in what counts as an 'acceptable' use of political power" (Mittiga 2021).

That is a nice way of saying that our individual rights and liberties will be gone for good.

What kinds of policies would a progressive government implement? As one possibility, Mittiga suggests that "governments might impel citizens to make significant lifestyle changes. One pertinent example concerns curbing meat-heavy diets, common in the Global North, given the enormous carbon footprint of animal agriculture" (Mittiga 2021). Good-bye Alberta beef, in other words.

Property rights will also be restricted so that governments can enact strict climate policies, especially for the energy and agriculture industries.

Objections to these policies may not be heard by other concerned citizens because Mittiga proposes the enactment of "a censorship regime that prevents the proliferation of climate denialism or disinformation in public media. This may well conflict with standard conceptions of freedom of expression or of the press" (Mittiga 2021).

Well, then, couldn't we simply elect new leaders to overturn these authoritarian policies? Nope. Mittiga wants a "litmus-test" for people seeking public office. Those who don't support the climate agenda are automatically disqualified. You must agree with government policies before being allowed to stand as a candidate.

And it gets even worse: "More strongly, governments may establish institutions capable of overturning previous democratic decisions (expressed, for example, in popular referenda or plebiscites) against the implementation of carbon taxes or other necessary climate policies" (Mittiga 2021).

You read that right: "democratic decisions" could be overturned by the authoritarian-progressive government. How is that different from a dictatorship?

Proposals of this kind would normally be published in obscure far-left periodicals that are unworthy of notice. But this one was published in the *American Political Science Review*, a flagship academic publication. Mittiga's scheme is worth understanding as an indication of the direction that some of our political elites would like to take us, and it ain't pretty.

For now, climate change is being used as the justification for reducing – and eventually eliminating – Alberta's oil and gas production. But if so-called "progressives" like Ross Mittiga get their way, it will be used for abolishing our historic rights and freedoms as well.

By becoming independent, Alberta's government would be able to protect its citizens, not only from a premature shutdown of its fossil fuel industries, but also from a dystopian future where we lose our freedoms and are ruled by a dictatorial "progressive" elite.

Conclusion

Of course, there will always be people who have objections to the idea of Alberta becoming independent. Fear of the consequences of such a change will be prominent among those objections. This is fair enough. Not everyone is going to be convinced.

The important point, though, is for citizens to consider the available information and arguments and make the best decisions for their future. The point of this book is to provide such information and show how it leads to the conclusion that Alberta independence is the best option.

Conclusion

It should be clear by now that Alberta has been severely mistreated within Canada, and that various attempts to rectify that problem were not successful. That lack of success was not the result of any fault in the people who worked hard for positive change. Instead, it was the result of Canada's political system. Ontario and Quebec together contain over half of Canada's population, so due to their voting power, they control all federal institutions.

Alberta – and even the four western provinces together – do not have the power to reform the country in a way that will provide redress for Alberta.

Braid and Sharpe explain the overall situation well:
> The problems go far beyond the abilities of any government to solve through tinkering or fiddling. They are rooted in the deepest structure of the country. Canada is a badly built nation – the only democratic federation in the western world in which every important institution, from the Supreme Court to the Senate, is dominated by the population centres. The largest provinces enjoy a multiple majority that spills

into every level of federal government (Braid and Sharpe 1990, 6).

Writing way back in 1990 as they were, Braid and Sharpe thought that Canada could be fixed. They wrote, "What the provinces need are the tools to fight for themselves, at the centre of power, on an equal regional footing – the tools of self-respect. The obvious first step is an equal, elected, and effective Senate" (Braid and Sharpe 1990, 206).

Indeed, in 1990 the Reform Party of Canada was growing by leaps and bounds in western Canada on a platform of "the West wants in," with a Triple-E Senate as its centerpiece. As explained earlier in this book, the proposal for a Triple-E Senate was categorically rejected by central Canada. It won't fly. Something else is needed.

For at least 50 years Alberta has been the whipping boy of Confederation. This is the lesson of history. With that in mind, it's clear that only independence can solve the problem of Alberta's gross mistreatment within Canada.

With independence, Albertans could chart their own path to prosperity and self-determination. That's the way to go, and the path to independence is perfectly constitutional.

Secession Reference decision

In the wake of the 1995 Quebec referendum on independence, the federal government sent a reference case to the Supreme Court of Canada, asking the court to rule on whether – according to Canadian or international law – Quebec could unilaterally declare independence from Canada. In the Secession Reference decision of 1998, the court ruled that no, Quebec could not unilaterally declare independence.

But – and this is a very big but – if Quebec held a referendum on independence with a clear question, and a clear majority of people voted in favour, then the federal government would be obligated to negotiate with Quebec over that province's independence. In other words, according to the Supreme Court, Canada's constitutional law includes a legal and peaceful pathway for a province to separate, as long as the right process is followed.

University of Toronto political scientist Robert Schertzer points out that in denying Quebec the right to unilaterally secede from Canada, a roadblock was placed in the path of the separatist movement.

> However, that was not the end of the story:
> At the same time, the ruling that there is a constitutional duty to negotiate in good faith with a province seeking to secede lends the secessionist movement legitimacy, pushing the other parties in the federation to recognize the validity of Québec's position in the face of a positive vote to secede (rather than simply being intransigent). The legitimacy the court affords Québec's position in this regard also helps to mitigate the negative outcome for it in the form of the illegality of unilateral secession and the clarity mandate (i.e., while Québec cannot unilaterally secede, if its people declare they want to leave the federation, the other members of the system have to work to make that a reality in good faith) (Schertzer 2018, 78).

That is, the federal government and the other provinces must negotiate "in good faith," they must not be "intransigent," and they must work to make secession "a reality in good faith."

The bottom line is that Alberta can become independent by holding a successful referendum on independence. This would be a legal, constitutional and peaceful process.

The court provided the basic constitutional principles for secession, but left it to Parliament to spell out the details of the process. Therefore in 2000, Parliament passed the *Clarity Act* to clearly explain those details.

Nevertheless, some people claim that even if Alberta followed the proper legal process and fulfilled the terms necessary to pursue independence, the federal government would not allow Alberta to leave because Alberta is such a major source of its revenue.

However, such a view ignores political and constitutional reality.

According to the Supreme Court, the federal government would have no legal or constitutional justification to deny a province the right to pursue secession if a clear majority of the province's citizens voted for independence. As it explained in the Secession Reference decision, "The other provinces and the federal government would have no basis to deny the right of the government of Quebec to pursue secession should a clear majority of the people of Quebec choose that goal, so long as in doing so, Quebec respects the rights of others" ([1998] 2 S.C.R. 293-294).

One of the key factors in the success of secession would be international recognition. If other countries recognize a political community as independent, it will be treated as a legitimate entity in world affairs. Were the federal government to ignore a clear referendum result, the international community would frown on such a violation of Canada's own constitutional law. As a result, the province trying to secede would likely receive sympathy and support from the international community.

As the court put it, any political actor "that does not act in accordance with the underlying constitutional principles puts at risk the legitimacy of its exercise of its rights, and the ultimate acceptance of the result by the international community" ([1998] 2 S.C.R. 294). At the same time, "compliance by the seceding province with such legitimate obligations would weigh in favour of international recognition" ([1998] 2 S.C.R. 289).

In short, then, the "ultimate success of such a secession would be dependent on recognition by the international community, which is likely to consider the legality and legitimacy of secession having regard to, amongst other facts, the conduct of Quebec and Canada, in determining whether to grant or withhold recognition" ([1998] 2 S.C.R. 296).

Essentially, this means that if the federal government did not conduct itself in accordance with Canada's constitutional law, and arbitrarily denied a province its right to pursue secession in accordance with the Supreme Court's ruling, the international community would likely side with the seceding province. Independence would then be achieved as a result of international support. Democracy would prevail.

As mentioned, the Supreme Court denied the validity of a unilateral declaration of independence, but put in place a constitutional process for a province to achieve independence. If the federal government denies the validity of the latter, it has in effect denied the validity of the former as well. One way or another, the federal government will be forced to accept the legitimate democratic will of a province that wants to secede.

There's also another significant factor in Alberta's favour. In 2008, Kosovo unilaterally declared independence from Serbia. Soon afterwards, Canada recognized Kosovo as an independent country. In other words, Canada officially accepted the legitimacy of Kosovo's unilateral declaration of independence.

According to constitutional lawyer Milan Markovic, this puts the Canadian government in a conundrum. On the one hand, it won't recognize a unilateral declaration of independence from Quebec, but it will accept such a declaration from other jurisdictions. As Markovic puts it, "Canada must somehow reconcile its acceptance of Kosovo's secession based on such a declaration with its claim that a similar action by Quebec would be contrary to international law" (Markovic 2010).

By supporting a unilateral declaration of independence from a European entity, Canada has weakened its credibility in opposing secession movements at home in the eyes of the international community.

Additionally, in 2010 the World Court ruled that Kosovo's unilateral declaration of independence did not violate international law. Markovic writes that, "After the court's Kosovo decision, it is naive to believe that the Clarity Act will prevent Quebec from unilaterally declaring its independence from Canada" (Markovic 2010).

The bottom line is that Alberta's future is in the hands of its citizens. If Albertans want to remain in Canada, its political status will stay the same. But if they vote in a clearly-worded referendum for independence, negotiations for such an outcome will begin.

Were the federal government to ignore Canada's constitutional law in such a case, that would only make the need for independence even clearer: Who would want to stay in a country that was ruled by such a lawless anti-democratic government?

The path for Alberta's future is clear and it is peaceful. With a successful referendum on independence, Albertans will be put in the driver's seat and be able to determine the future of their own community.

Alberta independence is the best option

The federal government plans to have Alberta's oil and gas workers retrained for so-called "green" jobs. This process goes under the misleading name of "just transition." What it really means is politicians who were not elected by Albertans get to kill jobs in Alberta.

The fact that the leaders imposing the "transition" on Alberta were not elected by Albertans undermines the legitimacy of this policy. And the fact that the Supreme Court of Canada subverted Alberta's constitutional rights over its control of natural resources means there is no solution to this problem within Canada. Alberta needs to become independent to save itself.

The politician in charge of killing Alberta's energy jobs is Energy and Natural Resources Minister Jonathan Wilkinson, an MP from Vancouver. Other key leaders in this scheme include Minister of Environment and Climate Change Steven Guilbeault, an MP from Montreal, Deputy Prime Minister Chrystia Freeland, an MP from Toronto, and Prime Minister

Justin Trudeau, an MP from Montreal. These latter three were elected by people who live more than 3000 kilometers from Alberta. Wilkinson was elected by people living hundreds of kilometers from Alberta.

That is, the job losses are going to be inflicted by people who Albertans did not elect. This is a problem.

The idea of democracy is citizens get to choose their own leaders who will then govern in the best interests of those they represent. But in Canada, the distribution of population creates a situation where people who live in more heavily populated parts of the country, such as central Canada, get to elect politicians who receive virtually no support in less populated parts of the country — especially Alberta and Saskatchewan.

Since people living in places like Montreal, Toronto, and Vancouver want to end Alberta's fossil fuel production, they elect people to undertake that dirty work.

In a constitutional democracy like Canada this should not be a huge problem because in theory, the constitution protects the rights of the provinces that did not vote for the government. According to section 92(A) of Canada's constitution, each province has exclusive jurisdiction over the development and management of its natural resources. This seems clear enough.

Unfortunately, it's not. The Supreme Court of Canada ruled 6-3 in its *References re Greenhouse Gas Pollution Pricing Act* decision of March 2021 that Trudeau could impose his carbon tax on the whole country, thus undermining section 92(A)'s protections.

As Russell Brown — one of the three dissenting Supreme Court judges — correctly explained, Trudeau's carbon tax clearly violated the constitution. In his dissent he wrote,

> The Act's subject matter falls squarely within provincial jurisdiction. It cannot be supported by any source of federal legislative authority, and it is therefore ultra vires Parliament. This court, a self proclaimed "guardian of the constitution" should condemn, not endorse, the attorney general of Canada's leveraging of the importance of climate change – and the relative popularity of Parliament's chosen policy response – to fundamentally alter the division of powers analysis under ss. 91 and 92 of the Constitution Act, 1867 and, ultimately, the division of powers itself (References re Greenhouse Gas, 2021 SCC 11 at para 454).

Yes, the Supreme Court of Canada "fundamentally altered" the constitutional division of powers in favour of the Trudeau government by this decision. Alberta was essentially robbed of its exclusive jurisdiction over its own natural resources.

But there's more. As Brown went on to say, the Supreme Court's majority decision

> rejects our Constitution and re-writes the rules of Confederation. Its implications go far beyond the Act, opening the door to federal intrusion – by way of the imposition of national standards – into all areas of provincial jurisdiction, including intra-provincial trade and commerce, health, and the management of natural resources (References re Greenhouse Gas, 2021 SCC 11 at para 456).

Read that again – "all areas of provincial jurisdiction" – are now under the threat of "federal intrusion."

Shortly after the manuscript of this book was completed, on October 13, 2023 the Supreme Court of Canada surprised the country by declaring much of the *Impact Assessment Act* to be unconstitutional. This was the law many Albertans referred to as the "no more pipelines act" because it gave the federal government authority to prohibit the construction of new pipelines for spurious reasons. Most observers expected the Supreme Court to uphold the law, which would strengthen Ottawa's death grip on Alberta's economy.

The court's decision is, in fact, a genuine victory for Alberta. However, it is only one battle in the long conflict between Alberta and the federal government. That conflict continues as before. In the aftermath of the decision, the federal government indicated that it will simply tweak the *Impact Assessment Act* to comply with the Supreme Court's opinion.

Besides that, the federal government doesn't see the court's decision quite the same way as it's viewed in Alberta. After the ruling was announced, "federal Environment Minister Steven Guilbeault and Natural Resources Minister Jonathan Wilkinson cautioned that the Supreme Court gave an advisory opinion, and their law is not struck down – adding that the concerns can be dealt with in a 'surgical way'" (Cryderman 2023, B6).

So while it's true Alberta won this round, the fight is far from over. Federal cabinet ministers are already scheming to limit the extent of Alberta's victory.

Alberta's future in Albertans' hands

If Alberta became independent, it could elect leaders who governed in the best interests of Albertans, not according to the "progressive" ideology of people in Montreal, Toronto and Vancouver. Politicians elected by Albertans would be enthusiastic champions of the energy industry and its workers.

Currently, though, we are at the mercy of leaders we did not elect who mean to harm us. And sometimes the Supreme Court itself is complicit in the undermining of our constitutional protections.

Of course, right now many Albertans have placed their hope in Danielle Smith's *Alberta Sovereignty Within a United Canada Act* that was passed in November 2022. I do not think their hopes will be realized.

There is a debate over whether the *Act* is constitutional or not. If it is constitutional, as Danielle Smith says, then it hasn't gotten anything for Alberta that we didn't have already.

But if it's unconstitutional, as many critics say, then using the *Alberta Sovereignty Within a United Canada Act* will result in the federal government challenging Alberta in court. This process could take many years, but it will end up at the Supreme Court of Canada where 7 of the 9 judges are from Eastern Canada. Clearly, Alberta's chances are not good.

Therefore, the *Alberta Sovereignty Within a United Canada Act* creates false hope and is unlikely to provide the leverage Alberta needs.

With all of this in mind, the choice is clear. We can allow politicians elected elsewhere to kill our jobs and our economy, or we can become independent and take our future into our own hands.

Alberta independence is the best option.

It's time for Alberta to leave Canada.

References

Aubin, Benoit. 2007. "Bill 101: 30 Years On." *The Canadian Encyclopedia.* https://www.thecanadianencyclopedia.ca/en/article/bill-101-30-years-on

Béland, Daniel, André Lecours, Gregory P. Marchildon, Haizhen Mou and M. Rose Olfert. 2017. *Fiscal Federalism and Equalization Policy in Canada: Political and Economic Dimensions.* North York, ON: University of Toronto Press.

Braid, Don, and Sydney Sharpe. 1990. *Breakup: Why the West Feels Left Out of Canada.* Toronto: Key Porter Books Limited.

Bratt, Duane. 2022. "Alberta conservatives look to Quebec model – but they may want to run the numbers again." *The Globe and Mail.* December 13. https://www.theglobeandmail.com/business/commentary/article-danielle-smiths-sovereignty-act-risks-turning-alberta-into-quebec-a/

Bramley-Moore, Alwyn. 1911. *Canada and Her Colonies: Or Home Rule for Alberta.* London: W. Stewart & Co.

Byfield, Ted. 1991. "The Reform party: The timing was right." In *Act of Faith: The Illustrated Chronicle of the Fastest-growing Political Movement in Canadian History: The Reform Party of Canada*. Terry O'Neill, ed. Vancouver: British Columbia Report Books.

Conway, John F. 2014. *The Rise of the New West: The History of a Region in Confederation*. Fourth edition. Toronto: James Lorimer & Company.

Cooper, Barry. 2009. *It's the Regime, Stupid!: A Report from the Cowboy West on Why Stephen Harper Matters*. Toronto: Key Porter Books.

Cooper, Barry. 2020. "Challenges for western independence." In *Moment of Truth: How to Think About Alberta's Future*, eds. Jack M. Mintz, Tom Flanagan, and Ted Morton, eds. Toronto: Sutherland House.

Crispo, John. 1979. *Mandate for Canada*. Don Mills, ON: General Publishing Co. Limited.

Cryderman, Kelly. 2023. "Court's ruling on environment act wasn't expected." *The Globe and Mail*. October 14: B6.

Dodek, Adam. 2015. "The Politics of the Senate Reform Reference: Fidelity, Frustration, and Federal Unilateralism." *McGill Law Journal*. Vol. 60, No. 4. June.

Ellis, Faron. 2005. *The Limits of Participation: Members and Leaders in Canada's Reform Party*. Calgary: University of Calgary Press.

Flanagan, Tom. 2011. "Re: 'Has the Centre Vanished?' by Stephen Clarkson." *Literary Review of Canada*. November: 30.

Foster, Peter. 1979. *The Blue-Eyed Sheiks: The Canadian*

Oil Establishment. Toronto: Collins Publishers.

Friesen, Gerald. 1999. *The West: Regional Ambitions, National Debates*. Toronto: A Penguin/McGill Institute book.

Gibbins, Roger. 1980. *Prairie Politics and Society: Regionalism in Decline*. Toronto: Butterworths.

Gibbins, Roger. 1981. "American Influence on Western Separatism." In *Western Separatism: The Myths, Realities & Dangers*. Edited by Larry Pratt and Garth Stevenson. Edmonton: Hurtig Publishers.

Gibbins, Roger. 1988. "Conservatism in Canada: The Ideological Impact of the 1984 Election." In *The Resurgence of Conservatism in Anglo-American Democracies*. Edited by Barry Cooper, Allan Kornberg, and William Mishler. Durham, NC: Duke University Press.

Gibbins, Roger. 1992. "Alberta and the National Community." In *Government and Politics in Alberta*, eds. Allan Tupper and Roger Gibbins. Edmonton: University of Alberta Press.

Gorman, Ruth. N.d. "How the Constitution Will Impoverish the West." Text of speech.

Gorman, Ruth. 1981. "Loss of 'important' rights feared under a changed constitution." *Calgary Herald*. February 3.

Graham, Ron. 1987. *One-Eyed Kings: Promise and Illusion in Canadian Politics*. Toronto: Totem Books.

Gray, Earle. 2000. *Forty Years in the Public Interest: A History of the National Energy Board*. Vancouver: Douglas & McIntyre Ltd.

Hiller, Harry H. 2002. "Region as a Social Construction." In *Regionalism and Party Politics in Canada*. Edited by Lisa

Young and Keith Archer. Don Mills, ON: Oxford University Press.

House, J. D. 1980. *The Last of the Free Enterprisers: The Oilmen of Calgary*. Toronto: Macmillan of Canada Limited.

Hoy, Claire. 1985. *Bill Davis: A Biography*. Agincourt, ON: Methuen Publications.

Hustak, Allan. 1979. *Peter Lougheed: A Biography*. Toronto: McClelland and Stewart Limited.

Jiang, Nathan. 2018. "A Review of Bill 101." *The Metric*. June 13. https://themetric.org/articles/a-review-of-bill-101

Koch, George. 1991. "To the western school of history, Canada was a business proposition." In *The Great West Before 1900*. Volume 1 of Alberta in the 20th Century. Edited by Ted Byfield. Edmonton: United Western Communications Ltd.

Manning, Preston. 1992. *The New Canada*. Toronto: Macmillan Canada.

Markovic, Milan. 2010. "What the Kosovo ruling means for Canada: trouble." *The Globe and Mail*. July 31. https://www.theglobeandmail.com/opinion/what-the-kosovo-ruling-means-for-canada-trouble/article1389913/

McDougall, Andrew. 2020. "Stuck in the Middle with You: Is the Trudeau Government Really Representative of a Central Canadian 'Laurentian Elite?'" *Canadian Studies*. December.

Melnyk, George. 1993. *Beyond Alienation: Political Essays on the West*. Calgary: Detselig Enterprises Ltd.

Mittiga, Ross. 2021. "Political Legitimacy,

Authoritarianism, and Climate Change." *American Political Science Review.* Published online December 6, 2021.

Morton, William L. 1980. *Contexts of Canada's Past: Selected Essays of W. L. Morton.* Edited by A. B. McKillop. Toronto: The Macmillan Company of Canada.

Nemeth, Tammy. 2006. "1980: Duel of the Decade." In *Alberta Formed Alberta Transformed*, Volume 2. Edited by Michael Payne, Donald Wetherell, and Catherine Cavanaugh. Edmonton: University of Alberta Press, and Calgary: University of Calgary Press.

Newman, Dwight, and Lorelle Binnion. 2015. "The Exclusion of Property Rights from the Charter: Correcting the Historical Record." *Alberta Law Review.* Vol 52, No 3.

Pannekoek, Frits. 2007. *Behind the Man: John Laurie, Ruth Gorman, and the Indian Vote in Canada.* Calgary: University of Calgary Press.

Ray, Don. 1984. "Western Separatism: Counter-elite of the marginalized." In *Stampede City: Power and Politics in the West.* Edited by Chuck Reasons. Toronto: Between the Lines.

Reference re Secession of Quebec, [1998] 2 S.C.R. 217.

References re Greenhouse Gas Pollution Pricing Act, 2021 SCC 11.

Reform Association of Canada. 1987. *A New Federal Political Party to Represent the West.* Edmonton: Reform Association of Canada.

Schertzer, Robert. 2018. "The Exemplar of the Secession Reference." In *Law, Politics, and the Judicial Process in Canada*, 4th Edition. Eds. F.L. Morton and Dave Snow. Calgary: University of Calgary Press.

Wood, David G. 1985. *The Lougheed Legacy*. Toronto: Key Porter Books Limited.

Zeihan, Peter. 2022. *The End of the World Is Just the Beginning: Mapping the Collapse of Globalization*. New York: HarperCollins Publishers.

About the Author

Michael Wagner is an independent researcher and writer, and a columnist for the Western Standard. He has a BA (Honours) and MA in political science from the University of Calgary and PhD in political science from the University of Alberta. He has previously written the books, *Alberta: Separatism Then and Now* and *No Other Option: Self-Determination for Alberta*. He and his wife have eleven children.

Once again Michael Wagner has made a compelling case for western Canadian independence, or at a minimum, far greater autonomy from Ottawa's overreach. We in the West must learn from the past 150+ years and end the never-ending cycle of abusive and invasive Liberal, and "better-for-the-west" Conservative, governments. The constitution isn't fair, and never will be. All that is necessary for this continual succession of abuse to prevail, is to do nothing!

> Hon. Jay Hill, Founder and original leader of the
>
> western-only Maverick Party

"Time to Leave sets out many obstacles Alberta faces within Canada from ever achieving an equal partnership or better deal with the self-interested Laurentian Elites, who have controlled Alberta since 1905. Alberta's interests have been and continue to be marginalized. In addition to our beleaguered history, succinctly stated by Wagner, including the influence of the self-proclaimed "progressive" Supreme Court of Canada, which has been adverse to Alberta, Canada has become a vassal state to unelected globalist and corporate organizations who do not have Alberta's interests in mind, yet dictate our domestic policies. It is for these reasons why Wagner is correct that it's time for Alberta to leave Canada and for Alberta to get out from under the yoke of Ottawa and the globalist agenda."

> Katherine Kowalchuk
> Interim Leader, The Independence Party of Alberta

Other books by this author:

No Other Option: Self-Determination for Alberta

In *No Other Option: Self-Determination for Alberta*, Michael Wagner explains that Alberta has been mistreated within Confederation for several decades. Albertans have tried to rectify this situation, but to no avail. Therefore, the best available option is for Alberta to become independent of Canada. Canadian constitutional law provides a pathway for provinces to become independent, so this can be done in a peaceful and legal manner. Following this option will provide Albertans with an opportunity to choose what's best for Alberta.

Alberta: Separatism Then and Now

In *Alberta: Separatism Then and Now*, Michael Wagner describes the origin and growth of the Alberta separatist movement. Prime Minister Pierre Trudeau played a very large role in pushing many Albertans into viewing independence as a credible alternative for the province. His attacks on Alberta's energy sector during the 1970s, and especially his National Energy Program of 1980, led to widespread concern about Alberta's place within Canada. It even resulted in the election of a separatist candidate in a 1982 by-election. This story is an important part of Alberta's recent history

www.ingramcontent.com/pod-product-compliance
Lightning Source LLC
Chambersburg PA
CBHW071718020426
42333CB00017B/2319